THE TEMPEST

THE TEMPEST
WILLIAM SHAKESPEARE

ILLUSTRATED BY
ARTHUR RACKHAM

GRAMERCY BOOKS
NEW YORK · AVENEL, NEW JERSEY

Preface and Compilation
Copyright © 1993 by Outlet Book Company, Inc.
All rights reserved

This 1993 edition is published by Gramercy Books
distributed by Outlet Book Company, Inc.,
a Random House Company,
40 Engelhard Avenue
Avenel, New Jersey 07001

The text used in this edition was
originally published in
The New Temple Shakespeare series,
edited by M.R. Ridley

Designed by Melissa Ring

Random House
New York • Toronto • London • Sydney • Auckland

Printed and bound in Singapore

Library of Congress Cataloging-in-Publication Data
Shakespeare, William, 1564–1616.
The tempest / by William Shakespeare.
p. :   ;   cm. — (Illustrated Shakespeare)
ISBN 0-517-09128-3
I. Title.   II. Series: Shakespeare, William, 1564–1616.
Illustrated Shakespeare.
PR2833.A1   1993   92-38749
822.3′3—dc20   CIP

8 7 6 5 4 3 2 1

PREFACE

Magical, ethereal, and wondrous are words often used to describe William Shakespeare's *The Tempest*. Samuel Taylor Coleridge, the English poet and eminent critic, described it as "almost miraculous." In no other of Shakespeare's plays, except *A Midsummer Night's Dream*—to which it is often compared—does he as prominently highlight and evoke the supernatural world.

The play focuses on Prospero, the deposed Duke of Milan, who is exiled on a remote island with his daughter, Miranda. He has, through the study and use of books on magic, attained an almost supreme command over nature and mankind. He uses his powers and that of his helper, the shape-changing sprite Ariel, to stage events which by play's end bring about the betrothal of his daughter to a prince and the return of his dukedom.

The Tempest is the last in a quartet of plays—the others are *Pericles, Cymbeline,* and *The Winter's Tale*—which represent Shakespeare's final creative period. In these works, often categorized as romances, he moved away from the real world and the grand passions of his histories and the great tragedies. They are characterized by an almost fairy tale quality, with settings in exotic or idyllic locales and plots revolving around improbable situations that often turn on fortuitous coincidence and resolve with good triumphing over evil.

Believed to be Shakespeare's last complete play, *The Tempest* is one of his finest achievements. He creates such memorable and enchanting characters as the monstrous Caliban, the ethereal Ariel, and the enigmatic Prospero. It also represents his final contemplations on the nature of reality, mankind, and evil. It is a play which leaves the audience questioning, for it is a work of sublime ambiguity. It has evoked numerous interpretations and has inspired many other works, including John Milton's *Comus*, Robert Browning's "Caliban Upon Setebos," and W. H. Auden's "The Sea and the Mirror." Even Mozart, shortly before his death, sketched an opera based on the play.

The Tempest is, perhaps, one of Shakespeare's most revealing works. Many critics have noted the unmistakable parallel between Prospero and the author himself. In Prospero's epilogue, "Now my charms are all o'erthrown, / And what strength I have's mine own," Shakespeare, the retiring playwright, and Prospero, the retiring magician, become almost indistinguishable. The line between illusion and reality fades as Shakespeare bids farewell to his art, the stage, and his audience, and he asks for one last round of applause.

Many of Shakespeare's plays were first published individually in Quarto editions that were later collected and published in Folio editions. But the only source for *The Tempest* is the first Folio edition of 1623. The text of this edition is the nearest possible approximation to what Shakespeare actually wrote. To avoid distraction, however, the spelling has been modernized. The punctuation adheres closely to the Elizabethan punctuation of the early text and, therefore, is often indicative of the way in which the lines are to be spoken.

This beautiful edition of *The Tempest* is illustrated by Arthur Rackham, the renowned English illustrator and watercolorist, who captures with delicacy of detail the wonderful magic of the play.

CHRISTOPHER MOORE

New York
1993

DRAMATIS PERSONÆ

ALONSO, *King of Naples.*
SEBASTIAN, *his brother.*
PROSPERO, *the right Duke of Milan.*
ANTONIO, *his brother, the usurping Duke of Milan.*
FERDINAND, *son to the King of Naples.*
GONZALO, *an honest old Counsellor.*
ADRIAN, } *Lords.*
FRANCISCO, }
CALIBAN, *a savage and deformed Slave.*
TRINCULO, *a Jester.*
STEPHANO, *a drunken Butler.*
Master of a Ship.
Boatswain.
Mariners.

MIRANDA, *daughter to Prospero.*

ARIEL, *an airy Spirit.*
IRIS,
CERES,
JUNO,   } *presented by Spirits.*
Nymphs,
Reapers,

Other Spirits attending on Prospero.

ACT I

SCENE 1

*On a ship at sea: a tempestuous noise of thunder and
lightning heard*

Enter a Ship-Master, and a Boatswain

Master. Boatswain!

Boatswain. Here, master: what cheer?

Master. Good; speak to the mariners: fall to 't, yarely,
or we run ourselves aground, bestir, bestir.   *Exit*

Enter Mariners

Boatswain. Heigh, my hearts, cheerly, cheerly, my
hearts! yare, yare! Take in the topsail. Tend to the
master's whistle. Blow till thou burst thy wind, if
room enough!

*Enter Alonso, Sebastian, Antonio, Ferdinand, Gonzalo,
and others*

Alonso. Good boatswain, have care: where's the
master? Play the men.

Boatswain. I pray now keep below.

Antonio. Where is the master, boatswain?

Boatswain. Do you not hear him? You mar our labour,
keep your cabins: you do assist the storm.

Gonzalo. Nay, good, be patient.

Boatswain. When the sea is. Hence! What cares these roarers for the name of king? To cabin; silence! trouble us not.

Gonzalo. Good, yet remember whom thou hast aboard.

Boatswain. None that I more love than myself. You are a counsellor, if you can command these elements to silence, and work the peace of the present, we will not hand a rope more, use your authority: if you cannot, give thanks you have liv'd so long, and make yourself ready in your cabin for the mischance of the hour, if it so hap. Cheerly, good hearts! Out of our way, I say.   *Exit*

Gonzalo. I have great comfort from this fellow: methinks he hath no drowning mark upon him, his complexion is perfect gallows: stand fast, good Fate, to his hanging, make the rope of his destiny our cable, for our own doth little advantage: if he be not born to be hang'd, our case is miserable.   *Exeunt*

Re-enter Boatswain

Boatswain. Down with the topmast! yare, lower, lower, bring her to: try with main-course. (*A cry within.*) A plague upon this howling! they are louder than the weather, or our office.

Re-enter Sebastian, Antonio, and Gonzalo

Yet again? what do you here? Shall we give o'er and drown, have you a mind to sink?

Sebastian. A pox o' your throat, you bawling, blasphemous, incharitable dog!

Boatswain. Work you then.

Antonio. Hang, cur, hang, you whoreson insolent noisemaker, we are less afraid to be drown'd than thou art.

Gonzalo. I'll warrant him for drowning, though the ship were no stronger than a nutshell, and as leaky as an unstanched wench.

Boatswain. Lay her a-hold, a-hold set her two courses off to sea again, lay her off.

Enter Mariners wet

Mariners. All lost, to prayers, to prayers, all lost!

Boatswain. What, must our mouths be cold?

Gonzalo. The king, and prince, at prayers! let's assist them,
For our case is as theirs.

Sebastian.   I'm out of patience.

Antonio. We are merely cheated of our lives by drunk-ards:
This wide-chopp'd rascal,—would thou might'st lie drowning
The washing of ten tides!

Gonzalo.   He'll be hang'd yet,
Though every drop of water swear against it,
And gape at wid'st to glut him.
(*A confused noise within:* 'Mercy on us!'—
'We split, we split!'—'Farewell my wife and chil-dren!'—
'Farewell, brother!'—'We split, we split, we split!')

Antonio. Let's all sink with the king.

Sebastian. Let's take leave of him.

Exeunt Antonio and Sebastian

Gonzalo. Now would I give a thousand furlongs of sea for an acre of barren ground; long heath, brown firs, any thing; the wills above be done; but I would fain die a dry death.   *Exeunt*

Scene II

The island. Before Prospero's cell

Enter Prospero and Miranda

Miranda. If by your art, my dearest father, you've
Put the wild waters in this roar, allay them:
The sky, it seems, would pour down stinking pitch,
But that the sea, mounting to the welkin's cheek,
Dashes the fire out. O, I have suffer'd
With those that I saw suffer! a brave vessel,
(Who had no doubt some noble creature in her)
Dash'd all to pieces! O, the cry did knock
Against my very heart! Poor souls, they perish'd.
Had I been any god of power, I would
Have sunk the sea within the earth, or ere
It should the good ship so have swallow'd, and
The fraughting souls within her.
Prospero.   Be collected,
No more amazement: tell your piteous heart
There's no harm done.
Miranda.   O, woe the day!
Prospero.   No harm.
I have done nothing but in care of thee,
(Of thee, my dear one, thee, my daughter) who
Art ignorant of what thou art, nought knowing
Of whence I am; nor that I am more better
Than Prospero, master of a full poor cell,
And thy no greater father.
Miranda.   More to know
Did never meddle with my thoughts.
Prospero.   'Tis time

I should inform thee farther. Lend thy hand,
And pluck my magic garment from me.—So,
                    Lays down his mantle
Lie there, my art: wipe thou thine eyes, have
  comfort,
The direful spectacle of the wreck, which touch'd
The very virtue of compassion in thee,
I have with such provision in mine art
So safely ordered, that there is no soil,
No, not so much perdition as an hair,
Betid to any creature in the vessel
Which thou heard'st cry, which thou saw'st sink.
  Sit down,
For thou must now know farther.
Miranda.   You have often
  Begun to tell me what I am, but stopp'd
  And left me to a bootless inquisition,
  Concluding 'Stay: not yet.'
Prospero.   The hour's now come;
  The very minute bids thee ope thine ear,
  Obey, and be attentive. Canst thou remember
  A time before we came unto this cell?
  I do not think thou canst, for then thou wast not
  Out three years old.
Miranda.   Certainly, sir, I can.
Prospero. By what? by any other house, or person?
  Of any thing the image tell me, that
  Hath kept with thy remembrance.
Miranda.   'Tis far off,
  And rather like a dream, than an assurance
  That my remembrance warrants. Had I not
  Four or five women once, that tended me?
Prospero. Thou hadst; and more, Miranda. But how is
  it

That this lives in thy mind? What seest thou else
In the dark backward and abysm of time?
If thou remember'st aught ere thou cam'st here,
How thou cam'st here thou mayst.
Miranda.   But that I do not.
Prospero. Twelve year since, Miranda, twelve year
    since,
Thy father was the Duke of Milan and
A prince of power.
Miranda.   Sir, are not you my father?
Prospero. Thy mother was a piece of virtue, and
She said thou wast my daughter; and thy father
Was Duke of Milan, and his only heir
A princess, no worse issued.
Miranda.   O the heavens,
What foul play had we, that we came from thence?
Or blessed was 't we did?
Prospero.   Both, both, my girl.
By foul play (as thou say'st) were we heav'd
    thence,
But blessedly holp thither.
Miranda.   O, my heart bleeds
To think o' the teen that I have turn'd you to,
Which is from my remembrance! Please you, farther.
Prospero. My brother and thy uncle, call'd Antonio,
(I pray thee, mark me, that a brother should
Be so perfidious!) he, whom next thyself
Of all the world I lov'd, and to him put
The manage of my state, as at that time
Through all the signories it was the first,
And Prospero the prime duke, being so reputed
In dignity; and for the liberal arts
Without a parallel; those being all my study,
The government I cast upon my brother,

And to my state grew stranger, being transported
And rapt in secret studies, thy false uncle
(Dost thou attend me?)
Miranda.   Sir, most heedfully.
Prospero. Being once perfected how to grant suits,
How to deny them; who to advance, and who
To trash for over-topping; new created
The creatures that were mine, I say, or changed 'em,
Or else new form'd 'em; having both the key,
Of officer, and office, set all hearts i' the state
To what tune pleas'd his ear, that now he was
The ivy which had hid my princely trunk,
And suck'd my verdure out on 't. Thou attend'st
    not.
Miranda. O, good sir, I do.
Prospero.   I pray thee, mark me:
I, thus neglecting worldly ends, all dedicated
To closeness, and the bettering of my mind
With that which, but by being so retir'd,
O'er-priz'd all popular rate, in my false brother
Awak'd an evil nature, and my trust,
Like a good parent, did beget of him
A falsehood in its contrary, as great
As my trust was, which had indeed no limit,
A confidence sans bound. He being thus lorded,
Not only with what my revenue yielded,
But what my power might else exact, like one
Who having into truth, by telling of it,
Made such a sinner of his memory
To credit his own lie, he did believe
He was indeed the duke, out o' the substitution
And executing the outward face of royalty
With all prerogative: hence his ambition growing,—
Dost thou hear?

Miranda.   Your tale, sir, would cure deafness.
Prospero. To have no screen between this part he
    play'd
And him he play'd it for, he needs will be
Absolute Milan. Me (poor man) my library
Was dukedom large enough: of temporal royalties
He thinks me now incapable; confederates
(So dry he was for sway) wi' the King of Naples
To give him annual tribute, do him homage,
Subject his coronet to his crown, and bend
The dukedom yet unbow'd,—(alas, poor Milan!)
To most ignoble stooping.
Miranda.   O the heavens!
Prospero. Mark his condition, and the event, then tell
    me
If this might be a brother.
Miranda.   I should sin
To think but nobly of my grandmother,
Good wombs have borne bad sons.
Prospero.   Now the condition.
This King of Naples, being an enemy
To me inveterate, hearkens my brother's suit,
Which was, that he, in lieu o' the premises
Of homage, and I know not how much tribute,
Should presently extirpate me and mine
Out of the dukedom, and confer fair Milan,
With all the honours, on my brother: whereon,
A treacherous army levied, one midnight
Fated to the purpose, did Antonio open
The gates of Milan, and, i' the dead of darkness,
The ministers for the purpose hurried thence
Me, and thy crying self.
Miranda.   Alack, for pity!
I, not remembering how I cried out then,

Will cry it o'er again: it is a hint
That wrings mine eyes to 't.
Prospero.   Hear a little further,
And then I'll bring thee to the present business
Which now's upon 's; without the which, this story
Were most impertinent.
Miranda.   Wherefore did they not
That hour destroy us?
Prospero.   Well demanded, wench:
My tale provokes that question. Dear, they durst
  not,
So dear the love my people bore me; nor set
A mark so bloody on the business; but
With colours fairer painted their foul ends.
In few, they hurried us aboard a bark,
Bore us some leagues to sea, where they prepar'd
A rotten carcass of a butt, not rigg'd,
Nor tackle, sail, nor mast, the very rats
Instinctively have quit it: there they hoist us,
To cry to the sea, that roar'd to us; to sigh
To the winds, whose pity, sighing back again,
Did us but loving wrong.
Miranda.   Alack, what trouble
Was I then to you!
Prospero.   O, a cherubin
Thou wast that did preserve me; thou didst smile,
Infused with a fortitude from heaven,
When I have deck'd the sea with drops full salt,
Under my burthen groan'd, which rais'd in me
An undergoing stomach, to bear up
Against what should ensue.
Miranda.   How came we ashore?
Prospero. By Providence divine,

Some food we had, and some fresh water, that
A noble Neapolitan, Gonzalo,
Out of his charity, (who being then appointed
Master of this design) did give us, with
Rich garments, linens, stuffs, and necessaries,
Which since have steaded much; so, of his
  gentleness,
Knowing I lov'd my books, he furnish'd me
From mine own library with volumes that
I prize above my dukedom.
Miranda.   Would I might
But ever see that man!
Prospero.   Now I arise, *Resumes his mantle*
Sit still, and hear the last of our sea-sorrow:
Here in this island we arriv'd, and here
Have I, thy schoolmaster, made thee more profit
Than other princes can, that have more time
For vainer hours; and tutors not so careful.
Miranda. Heavens thank you for 't! And now, I pray
  you, sir,
For still 'tis beating in my mind; your reason
For raising this sea-storm?
Prospero.   Know thus far forth;
By accident most strange, bountiful Fortune
(Now my dear lady) hath mine enemies
Brought to this shore; and by my prescience
I find my zenith doth depend upon
A most auspicious star, whose influence
If now I court not, but omit, my fortunes
Will ever after droop. Here cease more questions,
Thou art inclin'd to sleep; 'tis a good dulness,
And give it way: I know thou canst not choose.
                              Miranda sleeps

Come away, servant, come; I am ready now,
Approach, my Ariel: come.

Enter Ariel

Ariel. All hail, great master, grave sir, hail! I come
To answer thy best pleasure; be 't to fly,
To swim, to dive into the fire; to ride
On the curl'd clouds; to thy strong bidding, task
Ariel, and all his quality.
Prospero.   Hast thou, spirit,
Perform'd to point the tempest that I bade thee?
Ariel. To every article.
I boarded the king's ship; now on the beak,
Now in the waist, the deck, in every cabin,
I flam'd amazement, sometime I'ld divide
And burn in many places; on the topmast,
The yards and bowsprit, would I flame distinctly,
Then meet, and join. Jove's lightning, the precursors
O' the dreadful thunder-claps, more momentary
And sight-outrunning were not; the fire, and cracks
Of sulphurous roaring, the most mighty Neptune
Seem'd to besiege, and make his bold waves tremble,
Yea, his dread trident shake.
Prospero.   My brave spirit,
Who was so firm, so constant, that this coil
Would not infect his reason?
Ariel.   Not a soul
But felt a fever of the mad, and play'd
Some tricks of desperation; all but mariners
Plung'd in the foaming brine, and quit the vessel,
Then all afire with me: the king's son, Ferdinand,
With hair up-staring (then like reeds, not hair)
Was the first man that leap'd; cried, 'Hell is empty,
And all the devils are here.'

Prospero. Why, that's my spirit!
But was not this nigh shore?
Ariel. Close by, my master.
Prospero. But are they, Ariel, safe?
Ariel. Not a hair perish'd;
On their sustaining garments not a blemish
But fresher than before: and as thou bad'st me
In troops I have dispers'd them 'bout the isle!
The king's son have I landed by himself,
Whom I left cooling of the air with sighs,
In an odd angle of the isle, and sitting
His arms in this sad knot.
Prospero. Of the king's ship,
The mariners, say how thou hast dispos'd,
And all the rest o' the fleet.
Ariel. Safely in harbour
Is the king's ship, in the deep nook, where once
Thou call'dst me up at midnight to fetch dew
From the still-vex'd Bermoothes, there she's hid;
The mariners all under hatches stow'd,
Who, with a charm join'd to their suffer'd labour,
I have left asleep: and for the rest o' the fleet
(Which I dispers'd) they all have met again,
And are upon the Mediterranean flote
Bound sadly home for Naples,
Supposing that they saw the king's ship wreck'd,
And his great person perish.
Prospero. Ariel, thy charge
Exactly is perform'd; but there's more work:
What is the time o' the day?
Ariel. Past the mid season.
Prospero. At least two glasses: the time 'twixt six and
now
Must by us both be spent most preciously.
Ariel. Is there more toil? Since thou dost give me pains,

Let me remember thee what thou hast promis'd,
Which is not yet perform'd me.

Prospero.   How now? moody?
What is 't thou canst demand?

Ariel.   My liberty.

Prospero. Before the time be out? no more!

Ariel.   I prithee,
Remember I have done thee worthy service,
Told thee no lies, made thee no mistakings, serv'd
Without or grudge, or grumblings; thou didst
    promise
To bate me a full year.

Prospero.   Dost thou forget
From what a torment I did free thee?

Ariel.   No.

Prospero. Thou dost: and think'st it much to tread the
    ooze
Of the salt deep;
To run upon the sharp wind of the north,
To do me business in the veins o' the earth
When it is bak'd with frost.

Ariel.   I do not, sir.

Prospero. Thou liest, malignant thing! Hast thou forgot
The foul witch Sycorax, who with age and envy
Was grown into a hoop? hast thou forgot her?

Ariel. No, sir.

Prospero.   Thou hast: where was she born? speak;
    tell me.

Ariel. Sir, in Argier.

Prospero.   O, was she so? I must
Once in a month recount what thou hast been,
Which thou forget'st. This damn'd witch Sycorax,
For mischiefs manifold, and sorceries terrible
To enter human hearing, from Argier
Thou know'st was banish'd: for one thing she did

They would not take her life: is not this true?
Ariel. Ay, sir.
Prospero. This blue-eyed hag was hither brought with
  child,
And here was left by the sailors; thou my slave,
As thou report'st thyself, was then her servant,
And for thou wast a spirit too delicate
To act her earthy and abhorr'd commands,
Refusing her grand hests, she did confine thee,
By help of her more potent ministers,
And in her most unmitigable rage,
Into a cloven pine, within which rift
Imprison'd, thou didst painfully remain
A dozen years: within which space she died,
And left thee there: where thou didst vent thy
  groans
As fast as mill-wheels strike: then was this island
(Save for the son, that she did litter here,
A freckled whelp, hag-born) not honour'd with
A human shape.
Ariel.   Yes; Caliban her son.
Prospero. Dull thing, I say so: he, that Caliban
  Whom now I keep in service; thou best know'st
  What torment I did find thee in; thy groans
  Did make wolves howl, and penetrate the breasts
  Of ever-angry bears; it was a torment
  To lay upon the damn'd, which Sycorax
  Could not again undo: it was mine art,
  When I arriv'd, and heard thee, that made gape
  The pine, and let thee out.
Ariel.   I thank thee, master.
Prospero. If thou more murmur'st, I will rend an oak
  And peg thee in his knotty entrails, till
  Thou has howl'd away twelve winters.

Ariel.   Pardon, master,
I will be correspondent to command
And do my spiriting gently.
Prospero.   Do so: and after two days
I will discharge thee.
Ariel.   That's my noble master!
What shall I do? say what; what shall I do?
Prospero. Go make thyself like a nymph o' the sea, be
    subject
To no sight but thine and mine; invisible
To every eyeball else: go take this shape
And hither come in 't: go: hence with diligence!
                                        Exit Ariel
Awake, dear heart, awake, thou hast slept well;
Awake!
Miranda. The strangeness of your story put
    Heaviness in me.
Prospero.   Shake it off: come on,
We'll visit Caliban, my slave, who never
Yields us kind answer.
Miranda.   'Tis a villain, sir,
I do not love to look on.
Prospero.   But, as 'tis,
We cannot miss him: he does make our fire,
Fetch in our wood, and serves in offices
That profit us. What, ho! slave! Caliban!
Thou earth, thou! speak.
Caliban.   (*within*) There's wood enough within.
Prospero. Come forth, I say, there's other business for
    thee:
Come, thou tortoise! when?

              Re-enter Ariel like a water-nymph

Fine apparition! My quaint Ariel,

Hark in thine ear.

Ariel. My lord, it shall be done. *Exit*

Prospero. Thou poisonous slave, got by the devil himself
Upon thy wicked dam, come forth!

Enter Caliban

Caliban. As wicked dew as e'er my mother brush'd
With raven's feather from unwholesome fen
Drop on you both! a south-west blow on ye,
And blister you all o'er!

Prospero. For this, be sure, to-night thou shalt have
cramps,
Side-stitches, that shall pen thy breath up; urchins
Shall, for that vast of night that they may work,
All exercise on thee; thou shalt be pinch'd
As thick as honeycomb, each pinch more stinging
Than bees that made 'em.

Caliban. I must eat my dinner:
This island's mine by Sycorax my mother,
Which thou tak'st from me. When thou camest first,
Thou strok'st me, and made much of me; wouldst
give me
Water with berries in 't; and teach me how
To name the bigger light, and how the less,
That burn by day, and night: and then I lov'd thee,
And show'd thee all the qualities o' th' isle,
The fresh springs, brine-pits, barren place and
fertile:
Curs'd be I that I did so! All the charms
Of Sycorax, toads, beetles, bats, light on you!
For I am all the subjects that you have,
Which first was mine own king: and here you sty me
In this hard rock, whiles you do keep from me

The rest o' th' island.

Prospero.   Thou most lying slave,
Whom stripes may move, not kindness! I have us'd
    thee
(Filth as thou art) with human care, and lodg'd
    thee
In mine own cell, till thou didst seek to violate
The honour of my child.

Caliban. O ho, O ho! would 't had been done!
Thou didst prevent me; I had peopled else
This isle with Calibans.

Prospero.   Abhorred slave,
Which any print of goodness wilt not take,
Being capable of all ill! I pitied thee,
Took pains to make thee speak, taught thee each
    hour
One thing or other: when thou didst not, savage,
Know thine own meaning, but wouldst gabble, like
A thing most brutish, I endow'd thy purposes
With words that make them known. But thy vile
    race
(Though thou didst learn) had that in 't which good
    natures
Could not abide to be with; therefore wast thou
Deservedly confin'd into this rock, who hadst
Deserv'd more than a prison.

Caliban. You taught me language, and my profit on 't
Is, I know how to curse. The red plague rid you
For learning me your language!

Prospero.   Hag-seed, hence!
Fetch us in fuel and be quick thou'rt best
To answer other business. Shrug'st thou, malice?
If thou neglect'st, or dost unwillingly
What I command, I'll rack thee with old cramps,

Fill all thy bones with aches, make thee roar,
That beasts shall tremble at thy din.
Caliban. No, pray thee.
(*aside*) I must obey, his art is of such power,
It would control my dam's god, Setebos,
And make a vassal of him.
Prospero. So, slave, hence! *Exit Caliban*

Re-enter Ariel, invisible, playing and singing;
Ferdinand following

ARIEL'S SONG

Come unto these yellow sands,
And then take hands:
Courtsied when you have, and kiss'd
The wild waves whist:
Foot it featly here and there;
And, sweet sprites, the burthen bear.
Hark, hark!
Burthen (*dispersedly*). Bow-wow.
Ariel. The watch dogs bark:
Burthen (*dispersedly*). Bow-wow.
Ariel. Hark, hark! I hear
The strain of strutting chanticleer
Cry, Cock-a-diddle-dow.

Ferdinand. Where should this music be? i' th' air, or th'
earth?
It sounds no more: and sure it waits upon
Some god o' th' island. Sitting on a bank,
Weeping again the king my father's wreck,
This music crept by me upon the waters,
Allaying both their fury and my passion
With its sweet air: thence I have follow'd it,

(Or it hath drawn me rather) but 'tis gone.
No, it begins again.

Ariel sings

Full fathom five thy father lies,
    Of his bones are coral made;
Those are pearls that were his eyes,
    Nothing of him that doth fade,
But doth suffer a sea-change
Into something rich, and strange.
Sea-nymphs hourly ring his knell:
                    Burthen. Ding-dong
Ariel. Hark! now I hear them—Ding-dong, bell.

Ferdinand. The ditty does remember my drown'd
    father;
This is no mortal business, nor no sound
That the earth owes:—I hear it now above me.
Prospero. The fringed curtains of thine eye advance,
    And say what thou seest yond.
Miranda.   What is 't? a spirit?
    Lord, how it looks about! Believe me, sir,
    It carries a brave form. But 'tis a spirit.
Prospero. No, wench, it eats, and sleeps, and hath such
    senses
    As we have; such. This gallant which thou seest
    Was in the wreck; and, but he's something stain'd
    With grief (that's beauty's canker) thou mightest
    call him
    A goodly person: he hath lost his fellows,
    And strays about to find 'em.
Miranda.   I might call him
    A thing divine, for nothing natural
    I ever saw so noble.

Prospero.   (*aside*) It goes on, I see,
As my soul prompts it: spirit, fine spirit, I'll free thee
Within two days for this.
Ferdinand.   Most sure the goddess
On whom these airs attend! Vouchsafe my prayer
May know if you remain upon this island,
And that you will some good instruction give
How I may bear me here: my prime request
(Which I do last pronounce) is (O you wonder)
If you be maid, or no?
Miranda.   No wonder, sir,
But certainly a maid.
Ferdinand.   My language! heavens!
I am the best of them that speak this speech,
Were I but where 'tis spoken.
Prospero.   How? the best?
What were thou, if the King of Naples heard thee?
Ferdinand. A single thing, as I am now, that wonders
To hear thee speak of Naples. He does hear me;
And that he does I weep: myself am Naples,
Who with mine eyes (never since at ebb) beheld
The king my father wreck'd.
Miranda.   Alack, for mercy!
Ferdinand. Yes, faith, and all his lords, the Duke of
        Milan
And his brave son being twain.
Prospero.   (*aside*) The Duke of Milan,
And his more braver daughter, could control thee,
If now 'twere fit to do 't. At the first sight
They have chang'd eyes. Delicate Ariel,
I'll set thee free for this. (*to Ferdinand.*) A word,
        good sir;
I fear you have done yourself some wrong: a word.
Miranda. Why speaks my father so ungently? This

Is the third man that e'er I saw; the first
That e'er I sigh'd for: pity move my father
To be inclin'd my way!
Ferdinand. O, if a virgin,
And your affection not gone forth, I'll make you
The queen of Naples.
Prospero. Soft, sir! one word more.
(*aside*) They are both in either's powers: but this
  swift business
I must uneasy make, lest too light winning
Make the prize light. (*to Ferdinand.*) One word
  more; I charge thee
That thou attend me: thou dost here usurp
The name thou ow'st not, and hast put thyself
Upon this island as a spy, to win it
From me, the lord on 't.
Ferdinand. No, as I am a man.
Miranda. There's nothing ill can dwell in such a
  temple:
If the ill spirit have so fair a house,
Good things will strive to dwell with 't.
Prospero. Follow me.
Speak not you for him; he's a traitor. Come,
I'll manacle thy neck and feet together:
Sea-water shalt thou drink; thy food shall be
The fresh-brook mussels, wither'd roots, and husks
Wherein the acorn cradled. Follow.
Ferdinand. No,
I will resist such entertainment, till
Mine enemy has more power.
          He draws, and is charmed from moving
Miranda. O dear father,
Make not too rash a trial of him, for
He's gentle, and not fearful.

Prospero.   What! I say,
My foot my tutor? Put thy sword up, traitor,
Who mak'st a show, but dar'st not strike; thy con-
    science
Is so possess'd with guilt: come, from thy ward,
For I can here disarm thee with this stick,
And make thy weapon drop.
Miranda.   Beseech you, father.
Prospero. Hence! hang not on my garments.
Miranda.   Sir, have pity,
I'll be his surety.
Prospero.   Silence! one word more
Shall make me chide thee, if not hate thee. What?
An advocate for an impostor? hush!
Thou think'st there is no more such shapes as he,
(Having seen but him and Caliban:) foolish
    wench,
To the most of men this is a Caliban,
And they to him are angels.
Miranda.   My affections
Are then most humble; I have no ambition
To see a goodlier man.
Prospero.   Come on, obey:
Thy nerves are in their infancy again,
And have no vigour in them.
Ferdinand.   So they are:
My spirits, as in a dream, are all bound up:
My father's loss, the weakness which I feel,
The wreck of all my friends, nor this man's threats,
To whom I am subdued, are but light to me,
Might I but through my prison once a day
Behold this maid: all corners else o' th' earth
Let liberty make use of; space enough
Have I in such a prison.

Prospero. (aside) It works. (*to Ferdinand.*) Come on.
  Thou hast done well, fine Ariel! (*to Ferdinand.*)
    Follow me.
  (*to Ariel.*) Hark what thou else shalt do me.
Miranda.   Be of comfort;
  My father's of a better nature, sir,
  Than he appears by 's speech: this is unwonted
  Which now came from him.
Prospero.   Thou shalt be as free
  As mountain winds; but then exactly do
  All points of my command.
Ariel.   To the syllable.
Prospero. Come, follow: speak not for him.   *Exeunt*

ACT II

SCENE I

Another part of the island

Enter Alonso, Sebastian, Antonio, Gonzalo,
Adrian, Francisco, and others

Gonzalo. Beseech you, sir, be merry; you have cause,
(So have we all) of joy; for our escape
Is much beyond our loss. Our hint of woe
Is common, every day, some sailor's wife,
The masters of some merchant, and the merchant,
Have just our theme of woe; but for the miracle,
(I mean our preservation) few in millions
Can speak like us: then wisely, good sir, weigh
Our sorrow with our comfort.

Alonso.   Prithee, peace.
Sebastian. He receives comfort like cold porridge.
Antonio. The visitor will not give him o'er so.
Sebastian. Look, he's winding up the watch of his wit, by and by it will strike.
Gonzalo. Sir,—
Sebastian. One: tell.
Gonzalo. When every grief is entertain'd that's offer'd, Comes to the entertainer—
Sebastian. A dollar.
Gonzalo. Dolour comes to him, indeed, you have spoken truer than you purpos'd.
Sebastian. You have taken it wiselier than I meant you should.
Gonzalo. Therefore, my lord,—
Antonio. Fie, what a spendthrift is he of his tongue!
Alonso. I prithee spare.
Gonzalo. Well, I have done: but yet,—
Sebastian. He will be talking.
Antonio. Which, of he or Adrian, for a good wager, first begins to crow?
Sebastian. The old cock.
Antonio. The cockerel.
Sebastian. Done. The wager?
Antonio. A laughter.
Sebastian. A match!
Adrian. Though this island seem to be desert,—
Sebastian. Ha, ha, ha!—So; you're paid.
Adrian. Uninhabitable, and almost inaccessible,—
Sebastian. Yet,—
Adrian. Yet,—
Antonio. He could not miss 't.
Adrian. It must needs be of subtle, tender, and delicate temperance.

Antonio. Temperance was a delicate wench.

Sebastian. Ay, and a subtle, as he most learnedly deliver'd.

Adrian. The air breathes upon us here most sweetly.

Sebastian. As if it had lungs, and rotten ones.

Antonio. Or, as 'twere perfum'd by a fen.

Gonzalo. Here is everything advantageous to life.

Antonio. True, save means to live.

Sebastian. Of that there's none, or little.

Gonzalo. How lush and lusty the grass looks! how green!

Antonio. The ground, indeed, is tawny.

Sebastian. With an eye of green in 't.

Antonio. He misses not much.

Sebastian. No; he doth but mistake the truth totally.

Gonzalo. But the rarity of it is, which is indeed almost beyond credit,—

Sebastian. As many vouch'd rarities are.

Gonzalo. That our garments, being, as they were, drench'd in the sea, hold notwithstanding their freshness and glosses, being rather new-dyed than stain'd with salt water.

Antonio. If but one of his pockets could speak, would it not say he lies?

Sebastian. Ay, or very falsely pocket up his report.

Gonzalo. Methinks our garments are now as fresh as when we put them on first in Afric, at the marriage of the king's fair daughter Claribel to the King of Tunis.

Sebastian. 'Twas a sweet marriage, and we prosper well in our return.

Adrian. Tunis was never grac'd before with such a paragon to their queen.

Gonzalo. Not since widow Dido's time.

Antonio. Widow? a pox o' that! How came that widow
in? widow Dido!

Sebastian. What if he had said 'widower Æneas' too?
Good Lord, how you take it!

Adrian. 'Widow Dido' said you? you make me study of
that: she was of Carthage, not of Tunis.

Gonzalo. This Tunis, sir, was Carthage.

Adrian. Carthage?

Gonzalo. I assure you, Carthage.

Antonio. His word is more than the miraculous harp.

Sebastian. He hath rais'd the wall, and houses too.

Antonio. What impossible matter will he make easy
next?

Sebastian. I think he will carry this island home in his
pocket, and give it his son for an apple.

Antonio. And sowing the kernels of it in the sea, bring
forth more islands.

Gonzalo. Ay.

Antonio. Why, in good time.

Gonzalo. Sir, we were talking, that our garments seem
now as fresh as when we were at Tunis at the marriage of your daughter, who is now queen.

Antonio. And the rarest that e'er came there.

Sebastian. Bate, I beseech you, widow Dido.

Antonio. O, widow Dido? ay, widow Dido.

Gonzalo. Is not, sir, my doublet as fresh as the first day
I wore it? I mean, in a sort.

Antonio. That sort was well fish'd for.

Gonzalo. When I wore it at your daughter's marriage?

Alonso. You cram these words into mine ears, against
The stomach of my sense. Would I had never
Married my daughter there! for, coming thence,
My son is lost, and, in my rate, she too,
Who is so far from Italy remov'd

I ne'er again shall see her. O thou mine heir
Of Naples and of Milan, what strange fish
Hath made his meal on thee?
Francisco.   Sir, he may live:
I saw him beat the surges under him,
And ride upon their backs; he trod the water,
Whose enmity he flung aside; and breasted
The surge most swoln that met him; his bold head
'Bove the contentious waves he kept, and oar'd
Himself with his good arms in lusty stroke
To the shore, that o'er his wave-worn basis bow'd,
As stooping to relieve him: I not doubt
He came alive to land:
Alonso.   No, no, he's gone.
Sebastian. Sir, you may thank yourself for this great
    loss,
That would not bless our Europe with your daugh-
    ter,
But rather loose her to an African;
Where she, at least, is banish'd from your eye,
Who hath cause to wet the grief on 't.
Alonso.   Prithee peace.
Sebastian. You were kneel'd to, and importun'd other-
    wise,
By all of us; and the fair soul herself
Weigh'd between loathness and obedience, at
Which end o' the beam should bow. We have lost
    your son,
I fear for ever: Milan and Naples have
Mo widows in them of this business' making
Than we bring men to comfort them:
The fault's your own.
Alonso.   So is the dear'st o' the loss.
Gonzalo. My lord Sebastian,

The truth you speak doth lack some gentleness,
And time to speak it in: you rub the sore,
When you should bring the plaster.
Sebastian.   Very well.
Antonio. And most chirurgeonly.
Gonzalo. It is foul weather in us all, good sir.
When you are cloudy.
Sebastian.   Foul weather?
Antonio.   Very foul.
Gonzalo. Had I plantation of this isle, my lord,—
Antonio. He'ld sow 't with nettle-seed.
Sebastian.   Or docks, or mallows.
Gonzalo. And were the king on 't, what would I do?
Sebastian. 'Scape being drunk for want of wine.
Gonzalo. I' the commonwealth I would by contraries
Execute all things; for no kind of traffic
Would I admit; no name of magistrate;
Letters should not be known; riches, poverty,
And use of service, none; contract, succession,
Bourn, bound of land, tilth, vineyard, none;
No use of metal, corn, or wine, or oil;
No occupation, all men idle, all;
And women too, but innocent and pure;
No sovereignty;—
Sebastian.   Yet he would be king on 't.
Antonio. The latter end of his commonwealth forgets
the beginning.
Gonzalo. All things in common nature should produce
Without sweat or endeavour: treason, felony,
Sword, pike, knife, gun, or need of any engine,
Would I not have; but nature should bring forth
Of it own kind, all foison, all abundance,
To feed my innocent people.
Sebastian. No marrying 'mong his subjects?

Antonio. None, man, all idle; whores and knaves.
Gonzalo. I would with such perfection govern, sir;
  To excel the golden age.
Sebastian.   'Save his majesty!
Antonio. Long live Gonzalo!
Gonzalo.   And,—do you mark me, sir?
Alonso. Prithee no more: thou dost talk nothing to me.
Gonzalo. I do well believe your highness, and did it to
  minister occasion to these gentlemen, who are of
  such sensible and nimble lungs that they always use
  to laugh at nothing.
Antonio. 'Twas you we laugh'd at.
Gonzalo. Who in this kind of merry fooling am noth-
  ing to you: so you may continue, and laugh at noth-
  ing still.
Antonio. What a blow was there given!
Sebastian. And it had not fallen flat-long.
Gonzalo. You are gentlemen of brave mettle; you
  would lift the moon out of her sphere, if she would
  continue in it five weeks without changing.

  Enter Ariel (invisible) playing solemn music

Sebastian. We would so, and then go a bat-fowling.
Antonio. Nay, good my lord, be not angry.
Gonzalo. No. I warrant you; I will not adventure my
  discretion so weakly. Will you laugh me asleep, for
  I am very heavy?
Antonio. Go sleep, and hear us.
            All sleep except Alonso, Sebastian,
                        and Antonio
Alonso. What, all so soon asleep? I wish mine eyes
  Would, with themselves, shut up my thoughts: I
  find
  They are inclin'd to do so.

Sebastian.   Please you, sir,
Do not omit the heavy offer of it:
It seldom visits sorrow; when it doth,
It is a comforter.
Antonio.   We two, my lord,
Will guard your person while you take your rest,
And watch your safety.
Alonso.   Thank you.—Wondrous heavy.
                    Alonso sleeps. Exit Ariel
Sebastian. What a strange drowsiness possesses them!
Antonio. It is the quality o' the climate.
Sebastian.   Why
Doth it not then our eyelids sink? I find not
Myself dispos'd to sleep.
Antonio.   Nor I, my spirits are nimble.
They fell together all, as by consent
They dropp'd, as by a thunder-stroke. What might,
Worthy Sebastian?—O, what might?—No more:—
And yet, methinks I see it in thy face,
What thou shouldst be: the occasion speaks thee,
    and
My strong imagination sees a crown
Dropping upon thy head.
Sebastian.   What? art thou waking?
Antonio. Do you not hear me speak?
Sebastian.   I do, and surely
It is a sleepy language; and thou speak'st
Out of thy sleep. What is it thou didst say?
This is a strange repose, to be asleep
With eyes wide open; standing, speaking, moving;
And yet so fast asleep.
Antonio.   Noble Sebastian,
Thou let'st thy fortune sleep—die, rather; wink'st
Whiles thou art waking.

Sebastian.   Thou dost snore distinctly,
There's meaning in thy snores.
Antonio. I am more serious than my custom: you
Must be so too, if heed me; which to do
Trebles thee o'er.
Sebastian.   Well, I am standing water.
Antonio. I'll teach you how to flow.
Sebastian.   Do so: to ebb
Hereditary sloth instructs me.
Antonio.   O,
If you but knew how you the purpose cherish
Whiles thus you mock it! how, in stripping it,
You more invest it! Ebbing men, indeed,
(Most often) do so near the bottom run
By their own fear, or sloth.
Sebastian.   Prithee say on:
The setting of thine eye and cheek proclaim
A matter from thee; and a birth, indeed,
Which throes thee much to yield.
Antonio.   Thus, sir:
Although this lord of weak remembrance, this,
Who shall be of as little memory
When he is earth'd, hath here almost persuaded
(For he's a spirit of persuasion, only
Professes to persuade) the king his son's alive,
'Tis as impossible that he's undrown'd,
As he that sleeps here swims.
Sebastian.   I have no hope
That he's undrown'd.
Antonio.   O, out of that 'no hope'
What great hope have you! no hope that way is
Another way so high a hope that even
Ambition cannot pierce a wink beyond,
But doubt discovery there. Will you grant with me

That Ferdinand is drown'd?

Sebastian. He's gone.

Antonio. Then, tell me,
Who's the next heir of Naples?

Sebastian. Claribel.

Antonio. She that is queen of Tunis; she that dwells
Ten leagues beyond man's life; she that from Naples
Can have no note, unless the sun were post,—
The man i' the moon's too slow,—till new-born
    chins
Be rough and razorable; she that from whom
We all were sea-swallow'd, though some cast again,
And (by that destiny) to perform an act
Whereof what's past is prologue; what to come,
In yours and my discharge.

Sebastian. What stuff is this? how say you?
'Tis true, my brother's daughter's queen of Tunis;
So is she heir of Naples, 'twixt which regions
There is some space.

Antonio. A space whose every cubit
Seems to cry out, 'How shall that Claribel
Measure us back to Naples? Keep in Tunis,
And let Sebastian wake.' Say, this were death
That now hath seiz'd them, why, they were no worse
Than now they are. There be that can rule Naples
As well as he that sleeps; lords that can prate
As amply and unnecessarily
As this Gonzalo; I myself could make
A chough of as deep chat. O, that you bore
The mind that I do! what a sleep were this
For your advancement! Do you understand me?

Sebastian. Methinks I do.

Antonio. And how does your content
Tender your own good fortune?

Sebastian.   I remember
You did supplant your brother Prospero.
Antonio.   True:
And look how well my garments sit upon me,
Much feater than before: my brother's servants
Were then my fellows, now they are my men.
Sebastian. But for your conscience?
Antonio. Ay, sir; where lies that? if 'twere a kibe,
'Twould put me to my slipper: but I feel not
This deity in my bosom: twenty consciences,
That stand 'twixt me and Milan, candied be they,
And melt ere they molest! Here lies your brother,
No better than the earth he lies upon,
If he were that which now he's like (that's dead),
Whom I, with this obedient steel (three inches of
  it)
Can lay to bed for ever; whiles you, doing thus,
To the perpetual wink for aye might put
This ancient morsel, this Sir Prudence, who
Should not upbraid our course. For all the rest,
They'll take suggestion, as a cat laps milk;
They'll tell the clock to any business that
We say befits the hour.
Sebastian.   Thy case, dear friend,
Shall be my precedent; as thou got'st Milan,
I'll come by Naples. Draw thy sword: one stroke
Shall free thee from the tribute which thou payest,
And I the king shall love thee.
Antonio.   Draw together;
And when I rear my hand, do you the like,
To fall it on Gonzalo.
Sebastian.   O, but one word.
                            They talk apart

Re-enter Ariel, invisible

Ariel. My master through his art foresees the danger
That you, his friend, are in, and sends me forth
(For else his project dies) to keep them living.
                    Sings in Gonzalo's ear

    While you here do snoring lie,
    Open-eyed conspiracy
      His time doth take.
    If of life you keep a care,
    Shake off slumber and beware:
      Awake, awake!

Antonio. Then let us both be sudden.
Gonzalo.   Now, good angels
  Preserve the king!   *They wake*
Alonso. Why, how now? ho, awake?—Why are you
  drawn?
Wherefore this ghastly looking?
Gonzalo.   What's the matter?
Sebastian. Whiles we stood here securing your repose,
Even now, we heard a hollow burst of bellowing
Like bulls, or rather lions: did 't not wake you?
It struck mine ear most terribly.
Alonso.   I heard nothing.
Antonio. O, 'twas a din to fright a monster's ear;
To make an earthquake! sure, it was the roar
Of a whole herd of lions.
Alonso.   Heard you this, Gonzalo?
Gonzalo. Upon mine honour, sir, I heard a humming,
And that a strange one too, which did awake me:
I shak'd you, sir, and cried: as mine eyes open'd,
I saw their weapons drawn:—there was a noise,
That's verily. 'Tis best we stand upon our guard;

Or that we quit this place: let's draw our weapons.
Alonso. Lead off this ground and let's make further
  search
For my poor son.
Gonzalo.   Heavens keep him from these beasts!
For he is sure i' th' island.
Alonso.   Lead away.
Ariel. Prospero my lord shall know what I have done;
So, king, go safely on to seek thy son.   *Exeunt*

SCENE II

Another part of the island

*Enter Caliban with a burden of wood. A noise
of thunder heard*

Caliban. All the infections that the sun sucks up
From bogs, fens, flats, on Prosper fall, and make him
By inch-meal a disease! his spirits hear me,
And yet I needs must curse. But they'll nor pinch,
Fright me with urchin-shows, pitch me i' the mire,
Nor lead me, like a firebrand, in the dark
Out of my way, unless he bid 'em; but
For every trifle are they set upon me,
Sometime like apes, that mow and chatter at me,
And after bite me; then like hedgehogs, which
Lie tumbling in my barefoot way, and mount
Their pricks at my footfall; sometime am I
All wound with adders, who with cloven tongues
Do hiss me into madness.

Enter Trinculo

Lo, now, lo!
Here comes a spirit of his, and to torment me
For bringing wood in slowly. I'll fall flat,
Perchance he will not mind me.

Trinculo. Here's neither bush nor shrub, to bear off
any weather at all; and another storm brewing, I
hear it sing i' the wind: yond same black cloud,
yond huge one, looks like a foul bombard that
would shed his liquor: if it should thunder as it did
before, I know not where to hide my head: yond
same cloud cannot choose but fall by pailfuls. What
have we here, a man, or a fish? dead or alive? A fish,
he smells like a fish; a very ancient and fish-like
smell; a kind of, not of the newest Poor-John. A
strange fish! Were I in England now, as once I was,
and had but this fish painted, not a holiday fool
there but would give a piece of silver: there would
this monster make a man; any strange beast there
makes a man: when they will not give a doit to relieve a lame beggar, they will lay out ten to see a
dead Indian. Legg'd like a man; and his fins like
arms: warm o' my troth: I do now let loose my
opinion; hold it no longer: this is no fish, but an
islander, that hath lately suffered by a thunderbolt.
(*Thunder.*) Alas, the storm is come again! my best
way is to creep under his gaberdine; there is no
other shelter hereabout: misery acquaints a man
with strange bed-fellows. I will here shroud till the
dregs of the storm be past.

Enter Stephano, singing: a bottle in his hand

Stephano.   I shall no more to sea, to sea,
                 Here shall I die a-shore,—

This is a very scurvy tune to sing at a man's funeral:
well, here's my comfort.   *Drinks*
(*sings*)
The master, the swabber, the boatswain, and I,
    The gunner, and his mate,
Lov'd Mall, Meg, and Marian, and Margery,
    But none of us car'd for Kate;
For she had a tongue with a tang,
    Would cry to a sailor, Go hang!
She lov'd not the savour of tar nor of pitch,
Yet a tailor might scratch her where'er she did itch.
    Then, to sea, boys, and let her go hang!
This is a scurvy tune too: but here's my comfort.
                                                    Drinks

Caliban. Do not torment me:—O!

Stephano. What's the matter? Have we devils here?
Do you put tricks upon 's with savages, and men of
Ind, ha? I have not scap'd drowning, to be afeard
now of your four legs; for it hath been said, As
proper a man as ever went on four legs cannot make
him give ground; and it shall be said so again, while
Stephano breathes at nostrils.

Caliban. The spirit torments me:—O!

Stephano. This is some monster of the isle with four
legs, who hath got, as I take it, an ague. Where the
devil should he learn our language? I will give him
some relief, if it be but for that: if I can recover
him, and keep him tame, and get to Naples with
him, he's a present for any emperor that ever trod
on neat's-leather.

Caliban. Do not torment me, prithee; I'll bring my
wood home faster.

Stephano. He's in his fit now; and does not talk after
the wisest; he shall taste of my bottle: if he have

never drunk wine afore, it will go near to remove
his fit. If I can recover him, and keep him tame, I
will not take too much for him; he shall pay for him
that hath him, and that soundly.

Caliban. Thou dost me yet but little hurt; thou wilt
anon, I know it by thy trembling: now Prosper
works upon thee.

Stephano. Come on your ways; open your mouth; here
is that which will give language to you, cat: open
your mouth; this will shake your shaking, I can tell
you, and that soundly: you cannot tell who's your
friend: open your chaps again.

Trinculo. I should know that voice: it should be—but
he is drown'd; and these are devils:—O defend me!

Stephano. Four legs and two voices; a most delicate
monster! His forward voice, now, is to speak well of
his friend; his backward voice is to utter foul
speeches, and to detract. If all the wine in my bottle
will recover him, I will help his ague. Come:—
Amen! I will pour some in thy other mouth.

Trinculo. Stephano!

Stephano. Doth thy other mouth call me? Mercy,
mercy! This is a devil, and no monster: I will leave
him, I have no long spoon.

Trinculo. Stephano! If thou beest Stephano, touch me,
and speak to me; for I am Trinculo; be not afeard,
thy good friend Trinculo.

Stephano. If thou beest Trinculo, come forth: I'll pull
thee by the lesser legs: if any be Trinculo's legs,
these are they. Thou art very Trinculo indeed! How
cam'st thou to be the siege of this moon-calf? can
he vent Trinculos?

Trinculo. I took him to be killed with a thunder-stroke.
But art thou not drown'd, Stephano? I hope, now,
thou art not drown'd. Is the storm overblown? I hid

me under the dead moon-calf's gaberdine, for fear
of the storm. And art thou living, Stephano? O
Stephano, two Neapolitans scap'd!

Stephano. Prithee, do not turn me about, my stomach
is not constant.

Caliban. (*aside*) These be fine things, an if they be
not sprites.
That's a brave god, and bears celestial liquor:
I will kneel to him.

Stephano. How didst thou scape? How cam'st thou
hither? swear, by this bottle, how thou cam'st
hither. I escap'd upon a butt of sack, which the
sailors heaved o'erboard, by this bottle, which I
made of the bark of a tree with mine own hands,
since I was cast ashore.

Caliban. I'll swear upon that bottle, to be thy true
subject, for the liquor is not earthly.

Stephano. Here; swear, then, how thou escapedst.

Trinculo. Swum ashore, man, like a duck: I can swim
like a duck, I'll be sworn.

Stephano. Here, kiss the book. Though thou canst
swim like a duck, thou art made like a goose.

Trinculo. O Stephano, hast any more of this?

Stephano. The whole butt, man: my cellar is in a rock
by the sea-side, where my wine is hid. How now,
moon-calf, how does thine ague?

Caliban. Hast thou not dropp'd from heaven?

Stephano. Out o' the moon, I do assure thee: I was
the man i' the moon, when time was.

Caliban. I have seen thee in her; and I do adore thee:
my mistress show'd me thee, and thy dog, and thy
bush.

Stephano. Come, swear to that; kiss the book: I will furnish it anon with new contents: swear.

Trinculo. By this good light, this is a very shallow monster! I afeard of him? A very weak monster! The man i' the moon? A most poor credulous monster! Well drawn, monster, in good sooth!

Caliban. I'll show thee every fertile inch o' th' island; and I will kiss thy foot: I prithee be my god.

Trinculo. By this light, a most perfidious and drunken monster! when 's god's asleep, he'll rob his bottle.

Caliban. I'll kiss thy foot; I'll swear myself thy subject.

Stephano. Come on, then; down, and swear.

Trinculo. I shall laugh myself to death at this puppy-headed monster. A most scurvy monster! I could find in my heart to beat him,—

Stephano. Come, kiss.

Trinculo. But that the poor monster's in drink. An abominable monster!

Caliban. I'll show thee the best springs; I'll pluck thee berries;
I'll fish for thee; and get thee wood enough.
A plague upon the tyrant that I serve!
I'll bear him no more sticks, but follow thee,
Thou wondrous man.

Trinculo. A most ridiculous monster, to make a wonder of a poor drunkard!

Caliban. I prithee let me bring thee where crabs grow;
And I with my long nails will dig thee pig-nuts;
Show thee a jay's nest, and instruct thee how
To snare the nimble marmoset; I'll bring thee
To clustering filberts, and sometimes I'll get thee
Young scamels from the rock. Wilt thou go with me?

Stephano. I prithee now lead the way without any more talking. Trinculo, the king and all our company else being drown'd, we will inherit here: here; bear my bottle: fellow Trinculo, we'll fill him by and by again.

Caliban. (*sings drunkenly*)
            Farewell, master; farewell, farewell!
Trinculo. A howling monster; a drunken monster!
Caliban.   No more dams I'll make for fish,
            Nor fetch in firing
                At requiring;
            Nor scrape trencher, nor wash dish:
                'Ban, 'Ban, Ca-caliban
            Has a new master:—get a new man.
Freedom, hey-day! hey-day, freedom! freedom, hey-day, freedom!

Stephano. O brave monster! Lead the way.   *Exeunt*

ACT III

SCENE I

Before Prospero's cell

Enter Ferdinand, bearing a log

Ferdinand. There be some sports are painful, and their
 labour
Delight in them sets off: some kinds of baseness
Are nobly undergone; and most poor matters
Point to rich ends. This my mean task
Would be as heavy to me as odious, but
The mistress which I serve quickens what's dead,
And makes my labours pleasures: O, she is
Ten times more gentle than her father's crabbed;
And he's compos'd of harshness. I must remove
Some thousands of these logs, and pile them up,

Upon a sore injunction: my sweet mistress
Weeps when she sees me work, and says, such base-
ness
Had never like executor. I forget:
But these sweet thoughts do even refresh my la-
bours,
Most busy lest, when I do it.

Enter Miranda; and Prospero at a distance, unseen

Miranda.   Alas, now, pray you,
Work not so hard: I would the lightning had
Burnt up those logs that you are enjoin'd to pile!
Pray set it down, and rest you: when this burns,
'Twill weep for having wearied you: my father
Is hard at study; pray now rest yourself,
He's safe for these three hours.
Ferdinand.   O most dear mistress,
The sun will set before I shall discharge
What I must strive to do.
Miranda.   If you'll sit down,
I'll bear your logs the while: pray give me that,
I'll carry it to the pile.
Ferdinand.   No, precious creature,
I had rather crack my sinews, break my back,
Than you should such dishonour undergo,
While I sit lazy by.
Miranda.   It would become me
As well as it does you; and I should do it
With much more ease; for my good will is to it,
And yours it is against.
Prospero.   Poor worm, thou art infected!
This visitation shows it.
Miranda.   You look wearily.

Ferdinand. No, noble mistress, 'tis fresh morning with
  me
When you are by at night. I do beseech you,—
Chiefly that I might set it in my prayers,—
What is your name?
Miranda.   Miranda.—O my father,
  I have broke your hest to say so!
Ferdinand.   Admir'd Miranda,
  Indeed the top of admiration, worth
  What's dearest to the world! Full many a lady
  I have ey'd with best regard, and many a time
  The harmony of their tongues hath into bondage
  Brought my too diligent ear: for several virtues
  Have I lik'd several women, never any
  With so full soul, but some defect in her
  Did quarrel with the noblest grace she ow'd,
  And put it to the foil: but you, O you,
  So perfect, and so peerless, are created
  Of every creature's best!
Miranda.   I do not know
  One of my sex; no woman's face remember,
  Save, from my glass, mine own; nor have I seen
  More that I may call men than you, good friend,
  And my dear father: how features are abroad
  I am skilless of; but, by my modesty
  (The jewel in my dower) I would not wish
  Any companion in the world but you;
  Nor can imagination form a shape,
  Besides yourself, to like of. But I prattle
  Something too wildly, and my father's precepts
  I therein do forget.
Ferdinand.   I am, in my condition,
  A prince, Miranda, I do think, a king,
  (I would not so) and would no more endure

This wooden slavery than to suffer
The flesh-fly blow my mouth. Hear my soul speak:
The very instant that I saw you, did
My heart fly to your service, there resides
To make me slave to it, and for your sake
Am I this patient log-man.
Miranda.   Do you love me?
Ferdinand. O heaven, O earth, bear witness to this
    sound,
And crown what I profess with kind event
If I speak true! if hollowly, invert
What best is boded me to mischief! I,
Beyond all limit of what else i' the world,
Do love, prize, honour you.
Miranda.   I am a fool
To weep at what I am glad of.
Prospero.   Fair encounter
Of two most rare affections! Heavens rain grace
On that which breeds between 'em!
Ferdinand.   Wherefore weep you?
Miranda. At mine unworthiness, that dare not offer
What I desire to give; and much less take
What I shall die to want. But this is trifling,
And all the more it seeks to hide itself,
The bigger bulk it shows. Hence, bashful cunning,
And prompt me, plain and holy innocence!
I am your wife, if you will marry me;
If not, I'll die your maid: to be your fellow
You may deny me, but I'll be your servant
Whether you will or no.
Ferdinand.   My mistress, dearest,
And I thus humble ever.
Miranda.   My husband, then?
Ferdinand. Ay, with a heart as willing

As bondage e'er of freedom: here's my hand.
Miranda. And mine, with my heart in 't: and now
  farewell
  Till half an hour hence.
Ferdinand.   A thousand thousand!
      Exeunt Ferdinand and Miranda severally
Prospero. So glad of this as they I cannot be,
  Who are surpris'd withal; but my rejoicing
  At nothing can be more. I'll to my book,
  For yet ere supper-time must I perform
  Much business appertaining.   *Exit*

SCENE II

Another part of the island

Enter Caliban, Stephano, and Trinculo

Stephano. Tell not me;—when the butt is out, we will
  drink water, not a drop before: therefore bear up,
  and board 'em. Servant-monster, drink to me.
Trinculo. Servant-monster? the folly of this island!
  They say there's but five upon this isle; we are three
  of them, if th' other two be brain'd like us, the state
  totters.
Stephano. Drink, servant-monster, when I bid thee,
  thy eyes are almost set in thy head.
Trinculo. Where should they be set else? he were a
  brave monster indeed, if they were set in his tail.
Stephano. My man-monster hath drown'd his tongue
  in sack: for my part, the sea cannot drown me, I
  swam, ere I could recover the shore, five-and-thirty

leagues off and on, by this light, thou shalt be my
lieutenant monster, or my standard.
Trinculo. Your lieutenant, if you list, he's no standard.
Stephano. We'll not run, Monsieur Monster.
Trinculo. Nor go neither; but you'll lie like dogs, and
yet say nothing neither.
Stephano. Moon-calf, speak once in thy life, if thou
beest a good moon-calf.
Caliban. How does thy honour? Let me lick thy shoe.
I'll not serve him, he is not valiant.
Trinculo. Thou liest, most ignorant monster, I am in
case to justle a constable. Why, thou debosh'd fish
thou, was there ever man a coward, that hath drunk
so much sack as I to-day? Wilt thou tell a monstrous
lie, being but half a fish, and half a monster?
Caliban. Lo, how he mocks me! wilt thou let him, my
lord?
Trinculo. 'Lord,' quoth he? That a monster should be
such a natural!
Caliban. Lo, lo, again! bite him to death, I prithee.
Stephano. Trinculo, keep a good tongue in your head:
if you prove a mutineer, the next tree! The poor
monster's my subject, and he shall not suffer indig-
nity.
Caliban. I thank my noble lord. Wilt thou be pleas'd
to hearken once again to the suit I made to thee?
Stephano. Marry, will I: kneel, and repeat it; I will
stand, and so shall Trinculo.

Enter Ariel, invisible

Caliban. As I told thee before, I am subject to a tyrant,
a sorcerer, that by his cunning hath cheated me of
the island.
Ariel. Thou liest.

Caliban. Thou liest, thou jesting monkey, thou:
I would my valiant master would destroy thee!
I do not lie.
Stephano. Trinculo, if you trouble him any more in 's
tale, by this hand, I will supplant some of your teeth.
Trinculo. Why, I said nothing.
Stephano. Mum then, and no more. Proceed.
Caliban. I say, by sorcery he got this isle;
From me he got it. If thy greatness will
Revenge it on him, (for I know thou darest
But this thing dare not,)
Stephano. That's most certain.
Caliban. Thou shalt be lord of it, and I'll serve thee.
Stephano. How now shall this be compass'd? Canst
thou bring me to the party?
Caliban. Yea, yea, my lord, I'll yield him thee asleep,
Where thou mayst knock a nail into his head.
Ariel. Thou liest, thou canst not.
Caliban. What a pied ninny's this! Thou scurvy patch!
I do beseech thy greatness give him blows,
And take his bottle from him: when that's gone,
He shall drink nought but brine, for I'll not show him
Where the quick freshes are.
Stephano. Trinculo, run into no further danger: inter-
rupt the monster one word further, and, by this
hand, I'll turn my mercy out o' doors, and make a
stock-fish of thee.
Trinculo. Why, what did I? I did nothing. I'll go
farther off.
Stephano. Didst thou not say he lied?
Ariel. Thou liest.
Stephano. Do I so? take thou that. (*Beats him.*) As
you like this, give me the lie another time.
Trinculo. I did not give the lie. Out o' your wits, and

hearing too? A pox o' your bottle! this can sack and drinking do. A murrain on your monster, and the devil take your fingers!

Caliban. Ha, ha, ha!

Stephano. Now, forward with your tale.—Prithee, stand farther off.

Caliban. Beat him enough: after a little time,
I'll beat him too.

Stephano. Stand farther: come, proceed.

Caliban. Why, as I told thee, 'tis a custom with him
I' th' afternoon to sleep: there thou mayst brain him,
Having first seiz'd his books; or with a log
Batter his skull, or paunch him with a stake,
Or cut his wezand with thy knife. Remember
First to possess his books; for without them
He's but a sot, as I am, nor hath not
One spirit to command: they all do hate him
As rootedly as I. Burn but his books.
He has brave utensils (for so he calls them)
Which, when he has a house, he'll deck withal.
And that most deeply to consider is
The beauty of his daughter; he himself
Calls her a nonpareil: I never saw a woman,
But only Sycorax my dam, and she;
But she as far surpasseth Sycorax
As great'st does least.

Stephano. Is it so brave a lass?

Caliban. Ay, lord, she will become thy bed, I warrant,
And bring thee forth brave brood.

Stephano. Monster, I will kill this man: his daughter and I will be king and queen,—save our graces!— and Trinculo and thyself shall be viceroys. Dost thou like the plot, Trinculo?

Trinculo. Excellent.

Stephano. Give me thy hand, I am sorry I beat thee; but, while thou liv'st, keep a good tongue in thy head.

Caliban. Within this half hour will he be asleep, Wilt thou destroy him then?

Stephano. Ay, on mine honour.

Ariel. This will I tell my master.

Caliban. Thou mak'st me merry; I am full of pleasure, Let us be jocund: will you troll the catch You taught me but while-ere?

Stephano. At thy request, monster, I will do reason, any reason,—Come on, Trinculo, let us sing. *Sings*
Flout 'em and scout 'em,
And scout 'em and flout 'em;
Thought is free.

Caliban. That's not the tune.
Ariel plays the tune on a tabor and pipe

Stephano. What is this same?

Trinculo. This is the tune of our catch, play'd by the picture of Nobody.

Stephano. If thou beest a man, show thyself in thy like- ness: if thou beest a devil, take 't as thou list.

Trinculo. O, forgive me my sins!

Stephano. He that dies pays all debts: I defy thee. Mercy upon us!

Caliban. Art thou afeard?

Stephano. No, monster, not I.

Caliban. Be not afeard, the isle is full of noises, Sounds, and sweet airs, that give delight, and hurt not:
Sometimes a thousand twangling instruments Will hum about mine ears; and sometime voices, That, if I then had wak'd after long sleep, Will make me sleep again, and then, in dreaming, The clouds methought would open, and show riches Ready to drop upon me, that, when I wak'd, I cried to dream again.

Stephano. This will prove a brave kingdom to me, where I shall have my music for nothing.
Caliban. When Prospero is destroy'd.
Stephano. That shall be by and by: I remember the story.
Trinculo. The sound is going away, let's follow it, and after do our work.
Stephano. Lead, monster, we'll follow. I would I could see this taborer, he lays it on.
Trinculo. Wilt come? I'll follow, Stephano. *Exeunt*

SCENE III

Another part of the island

Enter Alonso, Sebastian, Antonio, Gonzalo, Adrian,
Francisco, and others

Gonzalo. By 'r lakin, I can go no further, sir,
My old bones ache: here's a maze trod, indeed,
Through forth-rights, and meanders! By your patience,
I needs must rest me.
Alonso.   Old lord, I cannot blame thee,
Who am myself attach'd with weariness,
To the dulling of my spirits: sit down, and rest:
Even here I will put off my hope, and keep it
No longer for my flatterer: he is drown'd
Whom thus we stray to find, and the sea mocks
Our frustrate search on land. Well, let him go.

Antonio. (*aside to Sebastian*) I am right glad that he's
    so out of hope:
Do not, for one repulse, forego the purpose
That you resolv'd to effect.
Sebastian. (*aside to Antonio*) The next advantage
    Will we take thoroughly.
Antonio. (*aside to Sebastian*) Let it be to-night,
    For, now they are oppress'd with travel, they
    Will not, nor cannot use such vigilance
    As when they are fresh.
Sebastian. (*aside to Antonio*) I say to-night: no more.
                    Solemn and strange music
Alonso. What harmony is this?—My good friends,
    hark!
Gonzalo. Marvellous sweet music!

*Enter Prospero above, invisible. Enter several strange Shapes,
bringing in a banquet: they dance about it with gentle
actions of salutations; and, inviting the King, &c. to eat, they
depart*

Alonso. Give us kind keepers, heavens!—What were
    these?
Sebastian. A living drollery. Now I will believe
    That there are unicorns; that in Arabia
    There is one tree, the phœnix' throne, one phœnix
    At this hour reigning there.
Antonio.   I'll believe both;
    And what does else want credit, come to me,
    And I'll be sworn 'tis true: travellers ne'er did lie,
    Though fools at home condemn 'em.
Gonzalo.   If in Naples
    I should report this now, would they believe me?
    If I should say, I saw such islanders,

(For, certes, these are people of the island,)
Who, though they are of monstrous shape, yet, note,
Their manners are more gentle-kind than of
Our human generation you shall find
Many, nay, almost any.
Prospero.   (*aside*) Honest lord,
Thou hast said well; for some of you there present
Are worse than devils.
Alonso.   I cannot too much muse
Such shapes, such gesture, and such sound, express-
   ing
(Although they want the use of tongue) a kind
Of excellent dumb discourse.
Prospero.   (*aside*) Praise in departing.
Francisco. They vanish'd strangely.
Sebastian.   No matter, since
They have left their viands behind; for we have
   stomachs.
Will 't please you taste of what is here?
Alonso.   Not I.
Gonzalo. Faith, sir, you need not fear. When we were
   boys,
Who would believe that there were mountaineers
Dew-lapp'd like bulls, whose throats had hanging
   at 'em
Wallets of flesh? or that there were such men
Whose heads stood in their breasts? which now we
   find.
Each putter-out of five for one will bring us
Good warrant of.
Alonso.   I will stand to, and feed,
Although my last, no matter, since I feel
The best is past. Brother, my lord the duke,
Stand to, and do as we.

Thunder and lightning. Enter Ariel, like a harpy; claps his wings upon the table; and, with a quaint device, the banquet vanishes

Ariel. You are three men of sin, whom Destiny,
That hath to instrument this lower world,
And what is in 't, the never-surfeited sea
Hath caus'd to belch up you; and on this island,
Where man doth not inhabit, you 'mongst men
Being most unfit to live. I have made you mad;
And even with such-like valour men hang and
   drown
Their proper selves.

        Alonso, Sebastian, &c. draw their swords

              You fools, I and my fellows
Are ministers of Fate, the elements,
Of whom your swords are temper'd, may as well
Wound the loud winds, or with bemock'd-at stabs
Kill the still-closing waters, as diminish
One dowle that's in my plume: my fellow-ministers
Are like invulnerable. If you could hurt,
Your swords are now too massy for your strengths,
And will not be uplifted. But remember
(For that's my business to you) that you three
From Milan did supplant good Prospero,
Expos'd unto the sea (which hath requit it)
Him and his innocent child: for which foul deed,
The powers, delaying (not forgetting) have
Incens'd the seas and shores; yea, all the creatures,
Against your peace. Thee of thy son, Alonso,
They have bereft; and do pronounce by me
Lingering perdition (worse than any death
Can be at once) shall step by step attend

You and your ways, whose wraths to guard you
from,
Which here, in this most desolate isle, else falls
Upon your heads, is nothing but heart's-sorrow,
And a clear life ensuing.

*He vanishes in thunder; then, to soft music, enter the Shapes
again, and dance, with mocks and mows, and carrying out
the table*

Prospero. Bravely the figure of this harpy hast thou
Perform'd, my Ariel; a grace it had, devouring:
Of my instruction hast thou nothing bated
In what thou hadst to say: so, with good life
And observation strange, my meaner ministers
Their several kinds have done: my high charms
work,
And these mine enemies are all knit up
In their distractions: they now are in my power;
And in these fits I leave them, while I visit
Young Ferdinand (whom they suppose is drown'd)
And his and mine lov'd darling.   *Exit above*
Gonzalo. I' the name of something holy, sir, why stand
you
In this strange stare?
Alonso.   O, it is monstrous! monstrous!
Methought the billows spoke, and told me of it,
The winds did sing it to me; and the thunder
(That deep and dreadful organ-pipe) pronounc'd
The name of Prosper: it did bass my trespass,
Therefore my son i' th' ooze is bedded; and
I'll seek him deeper than e'er plummet sounded,
And with him there lie mudded.   *Exit*

Sebastian.   But one fiend at a time,
I'll fight their legions o'er.
Antonio.   I'll be thy second.
                    Exeunt Sebastian and Antonio
Gonzalo. All three of them are desperate: their great
    guilt
(Like poison given to work a great time after)
Now 'gins to bite the spirits. I do beseech you
(That are of suppler joints) follow them swiftly,
And hinder them from what this ecstasy
May now provoke them to.
Adrian.   Follow, I pray you.   *Exeunt*

ACT IV

SCENE I

Before Prospero's cell

Enter Prospero, Ferdinand, and Miranda

Prospero. If I have too austerely punish'd you,
Your compensation makes amends, for I
Have given you here a third of mine own life,
Or that for which I live; who once again
I tender to thy hand: all thy vexations
Were but my trials of thy love, and thou
Hast strangely stood the test: here, afore Heaven,
I ratify this my rich gift. O Ferdinand,
Do not smile at me, that I boast her off,
For thou shalt find she will outstrip all praise,
And make it halt behind her.
Ferdinand.   I do believe it
Against an oracle.
Prospero. Then, as my gift, and thine own acquisition
Worthily purchas'd, take my daughter: but
If thou dost break her virgin-knot, before
All sanctimonious ceremonies may
With full and holy rite be minister'd,
No sweet aspersion shall the heavens let fall
To make this contract grow; but barren hate,
Sour-eyed disdain, and discord shall bestrew
The union of your bed, with weeds so loathly
That you shall hate it both: therefore take heed,
As Hymen's lamps shall light you.

Ferdinand.   As I hope
For quiet days, fair issue and long life,
With such love as 'tis now, the murkiest den,
The most opportune place, the strong'st suggestion
Our worser genius can, shall never melt
Mine honour into lust, to take away
The edge of that day's celebration,
When I shall think, or Phœbus' steeds are founder'd,
Or Night kept chain'd below.
Prospero.   Fairly spoke;
Sit, then, and talk with her, she is thine own.
What, Ariel! my industrious servant, Ariel!

Enter Ariel

Ariel. What would my potent master? here I am.
Prospero. Thou, and thy meaner fellows, your last
    service
Did worthily perform; and I must use you
In such another trick. Go bring the rabble
(O'er whom I give thee power) here to this place:
Incite them to quick motion, for I must
Bestow upon the eyes of this young couple
Some vanity of mine art: it is my promise,
And they expect it from me.
Ariel.   Presently?
Prospero. Ay, with a twink.
Ariel.   Before you can say, 'come,' and 'go,'
          And breathe twice, and cry, 'so, so,'
          Each one, tripping on his toe,
          Will be here with mop and mow.
          Do you love me, master? no?
Prospero. Dearly, my delicate Ariel. Do not approach
    Till thou dost hear me call.
Ariel.   Well; I conceive. *Exit*
Prospero. Look thou be true; do not give dalliance

Too much the rein: the strongest oaths are straw
To the fire i' the blood: be more abstemious,
Or else, good night your vow!
Ferdinand.   I warrant you, sir,
The white cold virgin snow upon my heart
Abates the ardour of my liver.
Prospero.   Well.
Now come, my Ariel! bring a corollary,
Rather than want a spirit: appear, and pertly!
No tongue! all eyes! be silent.   *Soft music*

Enter Iris

Iris. Ceres, most bounteous lady, thy rich leas
Of wheat, rye, barley, vetches, oats, and pease;
Thy turfy mountains, where live nibbling sheep,
And flat meads thatch'd with stover, them to keep;
Thy banks with pioned and twilled brims,
Which spongy April at thy hest betrims,
To make cold nymphs chaste crowns; and thy
    broom-groves,
Whose shadow the dismissed bachelor loves,
Being lass-lorn; thy pole-clipt vineyard;
And thy sea-marge, sterile and rocky-hard,
Where thou thyself dost air;—the queen o' the sky,
Whose watery arch and messenger am I,
Bids thee leave these, and with her sovereign grace,
Here, on this grass-plot, in this very place,
To come and sport:—her peacocks fly amain:

Juno appears in her car above

Approach, rich Ceres, her to entertain.

Enter Ceres

Ceres. Hail, many-colour'd messenger, that ne'er
Dost disobey the wife of Jupiter;

Who, with thy saffron wings, upon my flowers
Diffusest honey-drops, refreshing showers,
And with each end of thy blue bow dost crown
My bosky acres and my unshrubb'd down,
Rich scarf to my proud earth;—why hath thy queen
Summon'd me hither, to this short-grass'd green?
Iris. A contract of true love to celebrate,
And some donation freely to estate
On the bless'd lovers.
Ceres.   Tell me, heavenly bow,
If Venus or her son, as thou dost know,
Do now attend the queen? Since they did plot
The means that dusky Dis my daughter got,
Her, and her blind boy's scandal'd company,
I have forsworn.
Iris.   Of her society
Be not afraid: I met her deity
Cutting the clouds towards Paphos; and her son
Dove-drawn with her: here thought they to have
    done
Some wanton charm upon this man and maid,
Whose vows are, that no bed-right shall be paid
Till Hymen's torch be lighted: but in vain;
Mars's hot minion is return'd again,
Her waspish-headed son has broke his arrows,
Swears he will shoot no more, but play with spar-
    rows,
And be a boy right out.
Ceres.   High'st queen of state,
Great Juno, comes; I know her by her gait.

Enter Juno

Juno. How does my bounteous sister? Go with me

To bless this twain, that they may prosperous be,
And honour'd in their issue.   *They sing:*

Juno.   Honour, riches, marriage-blessing,
        Long continuance, and increasing,
        Hourly joys be still upon you!
        Juno sings her blessings on you.

Ceres.   Earth's increase, foison plenty,
        Barns and garners never empty;
        Vines with clustering bunches growing;
        Plants with goodly burthen bowing;
        Spring come to you at the farthest
        In the very end of harvest!
        Scarcity and want shall shun you;
        Ceres' blessing so is on you.

Ferdinand. This is a most majestic vision, and
   Harmonious charmingly. May I be bold
   To think these spirits?
Prospero.   Spirits, which by mine art
   I have from their confines call'd to enact
   My present fancies.
Ferdinand.   Let me live here ever;
   So rare a wonder'd father and a wise
   Makes this place Paradise.
               Juno and Ceres whisper, and send
                    Iris on employment
Prospero.   Sweet, now, silence!
   Juno and Ceres whisper seriously;
   There's something else to do: hush, and be mute,
   Or else our spell is marr'd.
Iris. You nymphs call'd Naiads of the windring brooks,
   With your sedg'd crowns, and ever-harmless looks,

Leave your crisp channels, and on this green land
Answer your summons; Juno does command:
Come, temperate nymphs, and help to celebrate
A contract of true love; be not too late.

Enter certain Nymphs

You sunburn'd sicklemen, of August weary,
Come hither from the furrow, and be merry,
Make holiday; your rye-straw hats put on,
And these fresh nymphs encounter every one
In country footing.

Enter certain Reapers, properly habited: they join with the Nymphs in a graceful dance; towards the end whereof Prospero starts suddenly, and speaks; after which, to a strange, hollow, and confused noise, they heavily vanish

Prospero. (*aside*) I had forgot that foul conspiracy
Of the beast Caliban and his confederates
Against my life: the minute of their plot
Is almost come. (*to the Spirits.*) Well done! avoid;
    no more!
Ferdinand. This is strange: your father's in some pas-
    sion
That works him strongly.
Miranda.   Never till this day
Saw I him touch'd with anger, so distemper'd.
Prospero. You do look, my son, in a moved sort,
As if you were dismay'd: be cheerful, sir.
Our revels now are ended. These our actors,
(As I foretold you) were all spirits, and
Are melted into air, into thin air,
And like the baseless fabric of this vision,
The cloud-capp'd towers, the gorgeous palaces,

The solemn temples, the great globe itself,
Yea, all which it inherit, shall dissolve,
And like this insubstantial pageant faded,
Leave not a rack behind: we are such stuff
As dreams are made on; and our little life
Is rounded with a sleep. Sir, I am vex'd,
Bear with my weakness, my old brain is troubled:
Be not disturb'd with my infirmity;
If you be pleas'd, retire into my cell,
And there repose, a turn or two I'll walk,
To still my beating mind.
Ferdinand, Miranda. We wish your peace. *Exeunt*
Prospero. Come with a thought. I thank thee, Ariel:
come.

Enter Ariel

Ariel. Thy thoughts I cleave to, what's thy pleasure?
Prospero.   Spirit,
We must prepare to meet with Caliban.
Ariel. Ay, my commander, when I presented Ceres,
I thought to have told thee of it, but I fear'd
Lest I might anger thee.
Prospero. Say again, where didst thou leave these
varlets?
Ariel. I told you, sir, they were red-hot with drinking,
So full of valour, that they smote the air
For breathing in their faces; beat the ground
For kissing of their feet; yet always bending
Towards their project. Then I beat my tabor,
At which like unback'd colts they prick'd their ears,
Advanc'd their eyelids, lifted up their noses
As they smelt music, so I charm'd their ears,
That, calf-like, they my lowing follow'd, through

Tooth'd briers, sharp furzes, pricking goss, and
  thorns,
Which enter'd their frail shins; at last I left them
I' the filthy-mantled pool beyond your cell,
There dancing up to the chins, that the foul lake
O'erstunk their feet.
Prospero.   This was well done, my bird.
Thy shape invisible retain thou still:
The trumpery in my house, go bring it hither,
For stale to catch these thieves.
Ariel.   I go, I go.   *Exit*
Prospero. A devil, a born devil, on whose nature
Nurture can never stick; on whom my pains,
Humanely taken, all, all lost, quite lost;
And as with age his body uglier grows,
So his mind cankers. I will plague them all,
Even to roaring.

Re-enter Ariel, loaden with glistering apparel, &c.

Come, hang them on this line.

Prospero and Ariel remain, invisible
Enter Caliban, Stephano, and Trinculo, all wet

Caliban. Pray you, tread softly, that the blind mole
  may not
Hear a foot fall: we now are near his cell.
Stephano. Monster, your fairy, which you say is a
  harmless fairy, has done little better than play'd the
  Jack with us.
Trinculo. Monster, I do smell all horse-piss, at which
  my nose is in great indignation.
Stephano. So is mine. Do you hear, monster? If I
  should take a displeasure against you, look you,—
Trinculo. Thou wert but a lost monster.

Caliban. Good my lord, give me thy favour still,
Be patient, for the prize I'll bring thee to
Shall hoodwink this mischance: therefore speak
softly,
All's hush'd as midnight yet.
Trinculo. Ay, but to lose our bottles in the pool,—
Stephano. There is not only disgrace and dishonour
in that, monster, but an infinite loss.
Trinculo. That's more to me than my wetting: yet this
is your harmless fairy, monster.
Stephano. I will fetch off my bottle, though I be o'er
ears for my labour.
Caliban. Prithee, my king, be quiet. See'st thou here,
This is the mouth o' the cell: no noise, and enter:
Do that good mischief, which may make this island
Thine own for ever, and I, thy Caliban,
For aye thy foot-licker.
Stephano. Give me thy hand. I do begin to have
bloody thoughts.
Trinculo. O King Stephano! O peer! O worthy Ste-
phano! look what a wardrobe here is for thee!
Caliban. Let it alone, thou fool, it is but trash.
Trinculo. O, ho, monster! we know what belongs to a
frippery. O King Stephano!
Stephano. Put off that gown, Trinculo, by this hand,
I'll have that gown.
Trinculo. Thy grace shall have it.
Caliban. The dropsy drown this fool! what do you
mean
To dote thus on such luggage? Let's alone,
And do the murder first: if he awake,
From toe to crown he'll fill our skins with pinches,
Make us strange stuff.
Stephano. Be you quiet, monster. Mistress line, is

not this my jerkin? Now is the jerkin under the line:
now, jerkin, you are like to lose your hair, and prove
a bald jerkin.

Trinculo. Do, do; we steal by line and level, an 't like
your grace.

Stephano. I thank thee for that jest; here's a garment
for 't: wit shall not go unrewarded while I am king
of this country. 'Steal by line and level' is an excellent pass of pate; there's another garment for 't.

Trinculo. Monster, come, put some lime upon your
fingers, and away with the rest.

Caliban. I will have none on 't: we shall lose our time,
And all be turn'd to barnacles, or to apes
With foreheads villanous low.

Stephano. Monster, lay-to your fingers: help to bear
this away where my hogshead of wine is, or I'll turn
you out of my kingdom: go to, carry this.

Trinculo. And this.

Stephano. Ay, and this.

*A noise of hunters heard. Enter divers Spirits, in shape of
dogs and hounds, hunting them about; Prospero and Ariel
setting them on*

Prospero. Hey, Mountain, hey!

Ariel. Silver! there it goes, Silver!

Prospero. Fury, Fury! there, Tyrant, there! hark, hark!

                Caliban, Stephano, and Trinculo
                          are driven out

Go, charge my goblins that they grind their joints
With dry convulsions, shorten up their sinews
With aged cramps, and more pinch-spotted make
them
Than pard or cat o' mountain.

Ariel.   Hark, they roar!

Prospero. Let them be hunted soundly. At this hour
Lies at my mercy all mine enemies:
Shortly shall all my labours end, and thou
Shalt have the air at freedom: for a little
Follow, and do me service.   *Exeunt*

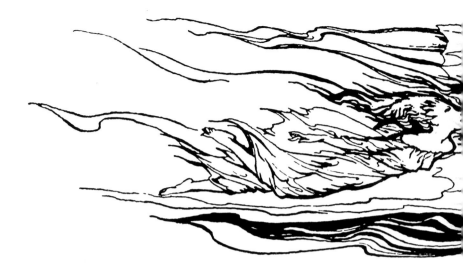

ACT V

SCENE I

Before the cell of Prospero

Enter Prospero, in his magic robes, and Ariel

Prospero. Now does my project gather to a head:
My charms crack not; my spirits obey, and time
Goes upright with his carriage. How's the day?
Ariel. On the sixth hour, at which time, my lord,
You said our work should cease.
Prospero.   I did say so,
When first I rais'd the tempest: say, my spirit,
How fares the king, and 's followers?
Ariel.   Confin'd together
In the same fashion as you gave in charge,
Just as you left them; all prisoners, sir,
In the line-grove which weather-fends your cell;
They cannot budge till your release. The king,
His brother, and yours, abide all three distracted,
And the remainder mourning over them,
Brimful of sorrow and dismay; but chiefly
Him that you term'd, sir, 'The good old lord,
    Gonzalo';

His tears runs down his beard, like winter's drops
From eaves of reeds. Your charm so strongly works
    'em,
That if you now beheld them, your affections
Would become tender.
Prospero.   Dost thou think so, spirit?
Ariel. Mine would, sir, were I human.
Prospero.   And mine shall.
Hast thou (which art but air) a touch, a feeling
Of their afflictions, and shall not myself,
One of their kind, that relish all as sharply,
Passion as they, be kindlier mov'd than thou art?
Though with their high wrongs I am struck to the
    quick,
Yet with my nobler reason 'gainst my fury
Do I take part: the rarer action is
In virtue than in vengeance: they being penitent,
The sole drift of my purpose doth extend
Not a frown further. Go, release them, Ariel,
My charms I'll break, their senses I'll restore,
And they shall be themselves.
Ariel.   I'll fetch them, sir.
                                                Exit
Prospero. Ye elves of hills, brooks, standing lakes, and
    groves,
And ye, that on the sands with printless foot
Do chase the ebbing Neptune, and do fly him
When he comes back; you demi-puppets, that
By moonshine do the green sour ringlets make,
Whereof the ewe not bites; and you, whose pastime
Is to make midnight mushrooms, that rejoice
To hear the solemn curfew, by whose aid
(Weak masters though ye be) I have bedimm'd
The noontide sun, call'd forth the mutinous winds,

And 'twixt the green sea, and the azur'd vault
Set roaring war: to the dread rattling thunder
Have I given fire, and rifted Jove's stout oak
With his own bolt; the strong-bas'd promontory
Have I made shake, and by the spurs pluck'd up
The pine and cedar: graves at my command
Have wak'd their sleepers, op'd, and let 'em forth
By my so potent art. But this rough magic
I here abjure; and, when I have requir'd
Some heavenly music (which even now I do)
To work mine end upon their senses, that
This airy charm is for, I'll break my staff,
Bury it certain fathoms in the earth,
And deeper than did ever plummet sound
I'll drown my book.   *Solemn music*

*Re-enter Ariel before: then Alonso, with a frantic gesture,
attended by Gonzalo; Sebastian and Antonio in like man-
ner attended by Adrian and Francisco: they all enter the
circle which Prospero had made, and there stand charmed;
which Prospero observing, speaks:*

A solemn air, and the best comforter
To an unsettled fancy, cure thy brains
(Now useless) boil within thy skull! There stand,
For you are spell-stopp'd.
Holy Gonzalo, honourable man,
Mine eyes, even sociable to the show of thine,
Fall fellowly drops. The charm dissolves apace;
And as the morning steals upon the night,
Melting the darkness, so their rising senses
Begin to chase the ignorant fumes that mantle
Their clearer reason. O good Gonzalo,
My true preserver, and a loyal sir
To him thou follow'st! I will pay thy graces

Home both in word and deed. Most cruelly
Didst thou, Alonso, use me and my daughter:
Thy brother was a furtherer in the act.
Thou art pinch'd for 't now, Sebastian. Flesh and
  blood,
You, brother mine, that entertain'd ambition,
Expell'd remorse and nature, who, with Sebastian
(Whose inward pinches therefore are most strong)
Would here have kill'd your king; I do forgive thee,
Unnatural though thou art. Their understanding
Begins to swell, and the approaching tide
Will shortly fill the reasonable shore,
That now lies foul and muddy. Not one of them
That yet looks on me, or would know me: Ariel,
Fetch me the hat and rapier in my cell,
I will discase me, and myself present
As I was sometime Milan: quickly, spirit,
Thou shalt ere long be free.

Ariel sings and helps to attire him

Where the bee sucks, there suck I,
In a cowslip's bell I lie,
There I couch when owls do cry.
On the bat's back I do fly
After summer merrily.
Merrily, merrily shall I live now
Under the blossom that hangs on the bough.

Prospero. Why, that's my dainty Ariel! I shall miss
  thee;
But yet thou shalt have freedom: so, so, so.
To the king's ship, invisible as thou art,
There shalt thou find the mariners asleep
Under the hatches; the master and the boatswain

Being awake, enforce them to this place,
And presently, I prithee.
Ariel. I drink the air before me, and return
Or ere your pulse twice beat.   *Exit*
Gonzalo. All torment, trouble, wonder and amazement
Inhabits here: some heavenly power guide us
Out of this fearful country!
Prospero.   Behold, sir king,
The wronged Duke of Milan, Prospero:
For more assurance that a living prince
Does now speak to thee, I embrace thy body;
And to thee and thy company I bid
A hearty welcome.
Alonso.   Whe'er thou be'st he or no,
Or some enchanted trifle to abuse me,
(As late I have been) I not know: thy pulse
Beats, as of flesh and blood; and, since I saw thee,
The affliction of my mind amends, with which,
I fear'd, a madness held me: this must crave—
An if this be at all—a most strange story.
Thy dukedom I resign, and do entreat
Thou pardon me my wrongs.—But how should
    Prospero
Be living, and be here?
Prospero.   First, noble friend,
Let me embrace thine age, whose honour cannot
Be measur'd or confin'd.
Gonzalo.   Whether this be
Or be not, I'll not swear.
Prospero.   You do yet taste
Some subtilties o' the isle, that will not let you
Believe things certain. Welcome, my friends all!
(*aside to Sebastian and Antonio.*) But you, my
    brace of lords, were I so minded,

I here could pluck his highness' frown upon you,
And justify you traitors: at this time
I will tell no tales.
Sebastian.   (*aside*) The devil speaks in him.
Prospero.   No.
For you, most wicked sir, whom to call brother
Would even infect my mouth, I do forgive
Thy rankest fault,—all of them; and require
My dukedom of thee, which perforce, I know,
Thou must restore.
Alonso.   If thou be'st Prospero,
Give us particulars of thy preservation,
How thou hast met us here, who three hours since
Were wreck'd upon this shore; where I have lost—
How sharp the point of this remembrance is!—
My dear son Ferdinand.
Prospero.   I am woe for 't, sir.
Alonso. Irreparable is the loss, and patience
Says it is past her cure.
Prospero.   I rather think
You have not sought her help, of whose soft grace
For the like loss I have her sovereign aid,
And rest myself content.
Alonso.   You the like loss?
Prospero. As great to me, as late; and, supportable
To make the dear loss, have I means much weaker
Than you may call to comfort you; for I
Have lost my daughter.
Alonso.   A daughter?
O heavens, that they were living both in Naples,
The king and queen there! that they were, I wish
Myself were mudded in that oozy bed
Where my son lies. When did you lose your
   daughter?

Prospero. In this last tempest. I perceive these lords
  At this encounter do so much admire,
  That they devour their reason, and scarce think
  Their eyes do offices of truth, their words
  Are natural breath: but, howsoe'er you have
  Been justled from your senses, know for certain
  That I am Prospero, and that very duke
  Which was thrust forth of Milan, who most
    strangely
  Upon this shore, where you were wreck'd, was
    landed,
  To be the lord on 't. No more yet of this,
  For 'tis a chronicle of day by day,
  Not a relation for a breakfast, nor
  Befitting this first meeting. Welcome, sir;
  This cell's my court: here have I few attendants,
  And subjects none abroad: pray you look in.
  My dukedom since you have given me again,
  I will requite you with as good a thing,
  At least bring forth a wonder, to content ye
  As much as me my dukedom.

  Here Prospero discovers Ferdinand and Miranda,
  playing at chess

Miranda. Sweet lord, you play me false.
Ferdinand.   No, my dear'st love,
  I would not for the world.
Miranda. Yes, for a score of kingdoms you should
    wrangle,
  And I would call it fair play.
Alonso.   If this prove
  A vision of the island, one dear son
  Shall I twice lose.
Sebastian.   A most high miracle!

Ferdinand. Though the seas threaten, they are
  merciful;
I have curs'd them without cause.   *Kneels*
Alonso.   Now all the blessings
  Of a glad father compass thee about!
  Arise, and say how thou cam'st here.
Miranda.   O, wonder!
  How many goodly creatures are there here!
  How beauteous mankind is! O brave new world,
  That has such people in 't!
Prospero.   'Tis new to thee.
Alonso. What is this maid, with whom thou wast at
  play?
  Your eld'st acquaintance cannot be three hours:
  Is she the goddess that hath sever'd us,
  And brought us thus together?
Ferdinand.   Sir, she is mortal;
  But, by immortal Providence, she's mine;
  I chose her when I could not ask my father
  For his advice; nor thought I had one. She
  Is daughter to this famous Duke of Milan,
  Of whom so often I have heard renown,
  But never saw before; of whom I have
  Receiv'd a second life; and second father
  This lady makes him to me.
Alonso.   I am hers:
  But, O, how oddly will it sound, that I
  Must ask my child forgiveness!
Prospero.   There, sir, stop,
  Let us not burthen our remembrance with
  A heaviness that's gone.
Gonzalo.   I have inly wept,
  Or should have spoke ere this. Look down, you
  gods,

And on this couple drop a blessed crown!
For it is you that have chalk'd forth the way
Which brought us hither.
Alonso.   I say, Amen, Gonzalo!
Gonzalo. Was Milan thrust from Milan, that his issue
Should become kings of Naples? O, rejoice
Beyond a common joy, and set it down
With gold on lasting pillars: In one voyage
Did Claribel her husband find at Tunis,
And Ferdinand, her brother, found a wife
Where he himself was lost; Prospero his dukedom
In a poor isle; and all of us ourselves,
When no man was his own.
Alonso. (*to Ferdinand and Miranda*) Give me your
    hands:
Let grief and sorrow still embrace his heart
That doth not wish you joy!
Gonzalo.   Be it so! Amen!

*Re-enter Ariel, with the Master and Boatswain
amazedly following*

O, look, sir, look, sir! here is more of us:
I prophesied, if a gallows were on land,
This fellow could not drown. Now, blasphemy,
That swear'st grace o'erboard, not an oath on shore?
Hast thou no mouth by land? What is the news?
Boatswain. The best news is, that we have safely
    found
Our king and company; the next, our ship—
Which, but three glasses since, we gave out split—
Is tight, and yare, and bravely rigg'd, as when
We first put out to sea.
Ariel. (*aside to Prospero*) Sir, all this service
Have I done since I went.

Prospero. (*aside to Ariel*) My tricksy spirit!

Alonso. These are not natural events, they strengthen
  From strange to stranger: say, how came you
    hither?

Boatswain. If I did think, sir, I were well awake,
  I'ld strive to tell you. We were dead of sleep,
  And (how we know not) all clapp'd under hatches,
  Where, but even now, with strange and several
    noises
  Of roaring, shrieking, howling, jingling chains,
  And mo diversity of sounds, all horrible,
  We were awak'd; straightway, at liberty;
  Where we, in all her trim, freshly beheld
  Our royal, good, and gallant ship; our master
  Capering to eye her:—on a trice, so please you,
  Even in a dream, were we divided from them,
  And were brought moping hither.

Ariel.   (*aside to Prospero*) Was 't well done?

Prospero. (*aside to Ariel*) Bravely, my diligence, thou
  shalt be free.

Alonso. This is as strange a maze as e'er men trod,
  And there is in this business more than nature
  Was ever conduct of: some oracle
  Must rectify our knowledge.

Prospero.   Sir, my liege,
  Do not infest your mind with beating on
  The strangeness of this business; at pick'd leisure
  (Which shall be shortly single) I'll resolve you,
  Which to you shall seem probable, of every
  These happen'd accidents; till when, be cheerful,
  And think of each thing well. (*aside to Ariel.*) Come
    hither, spirit,
  Set Caliban, and his companions free;

Untie the spell. (*exit Ariel.*) How fares my gracious
  sir?
There are yet missing of your company
Some few odd lads that you remember not.

> *Re-enter Ariel, driving in Caliban, Stephano, and
> Trinculo, in their stolen apparel*

Stephano. Every man shift for all the rest, and let no
  man take care of himself; for all is but fortune.—
  Coragio, bully-monster, coragio!
Trinculo. If these be true spies which I wear in my
  head, here's a goodly sight.
Caliban. O Setebos, these be brave spirits indeed!
  How fine my master is! I am afraid
  He will chastise me.
Sebastian.   Ha, ha!
  What things are these, my lord Antonio?
  Will money buy 'em?
Antonio.   Very like; one of them
  Is a plain fish, and, no doubt, marketable.
Prospero. Mark but the badges of these men, my lords,
  Then say if they be true. This mis-shapen knave,
  His mother was a witch, and one so strong
  That could control the moon; make flows, and ebbs,
  And deal in her command, without her power.
  These three have robb'd me, and this demi-devil
  (For he's a bastard one) had plotted with them
  To take my life. Two of these fellows you
  Must know and own, this thing of darkness I
  Acknowledge mine.
Caliban.   I shall be pinch'd to death.
Alonso. Is not this Stephano, my drunken butler?
Sebastian. He is drunk now; where had he wine?

Alonso. And Trinculo is reeling ripe: where should
  they
Find this grand liquor that hath gilded 'em?
How cam'st thou in this pickle?
Trinculo. I have been in such a pickle since I saw you
  last, that I fear me will never out of my bones: I shall
  not fear fly-blowing.
Sebastian. Why, how now, Stephano?
Stephano. O, touch me not;—I am not Stephano, but
  a cramp.
Prospero. You'ld be king o' the isle, sirrah?
Stephano. I should have been a sore one, then.
Alonso. This is a strange thing as e'er I look'd on.
                        Pointing to Caliban
Prospero. He is as disproportion'd in his manners
  As in his shape. Go, sirrah, to my cell,
  Take with you your companions; as you look
  To have my pardon, trim it handsomely.
Caliban. Ay, that I will; and I'll be wise hereafter,
  And seek for grace. What a thrice-double ass
  Was I to take this drunkard for a god,
  And worship this dull fool!
Prospero.   Go to, away!
Alonso. Hence, and bestow your luggage where you
  found it.
Sebastian. Or stole it, rather.
         Exeunt Caliban, Stephano, and Trinculo
Prospero. Sir, I invite your Highness, and your train
  To my poor cell; where you shall take your rest
  For this one night, which, part of it, I'll waste
  With such discourse as, I not doubt, shall make it
  Go quick away: the story of my life,
  And the particular accidents gone by
  Since I came to this isle: and in the morn

I'll bring you to your ship, and so to Naples,
Where I have hope to see the nuptial
Of these our dear-belov'd solemnized,
And thence retire me to my Milan, where
Every third thought shall be my grave.
Alonso.   I long
To hear the story of your life; which must
Take the ear strangely.
Prospero.   I'll deliver all,
And promise you calm seas, auspicious gales,
And sail so expeditious, that shall catch
Your royal fleet far off. (*aside to Ariel.*) My Ariel,
    chick,
That is thy charge: then to the elements
Be free, and fare thou well! Please you, draw near.
                                        Exeunt

EPILOGUE

Spoken by Prospero

Now my charms are all o'erthrown,
And what strength I have's mine own,
Which is most faint: now, 'tis true,
I must be here confin'd by you,
Or sent to Naples. Let me not,
Since I have my dukedom got,
And pardon'd the deceiver, dwell
In this bare island by your spell,
But release me from my bands
With the help of your good hands:
Gentle breath of yours my sails
Must fill, or else my project fails,
Which was to please. Now I want
Spirits to enforce, art to enchant,
And my ending is despair,
Unless I be reliev'd by prayer,
Which pierces so, that it assaults
Mercy itself, and frees all faults.
As you from crimes would pardon'd be,
Let your indulgence set me free.

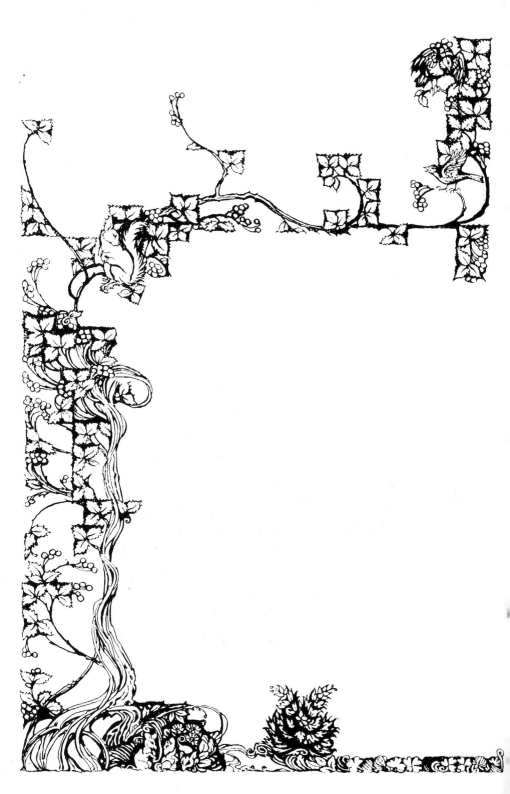